Tip-top

BEA

Great Britain's top 100 beaches

Stuart Kirby

studio **cactus**

First published in Great Britain in 2005 by

studio **cactus** ltd

13 SOUTHGATE STREET WINCHESTER HAMPSHIRE SO23 9DZ
TEL 01962 878600 FAX 01962 859278
E-MAIL MAIL@STUDIOCACTUS.CO.UK WEBSITE WWW.STUDIOCACTUS.CO.UK

Copyright © 2005 studio **cactus** ltd
Text Copyright © Stuart Kirby

ISBN 1-904239-06-4

A catalogue record for this book is
available from the British Library.

Printed in the UK by Short Run Press

Contents

Author's introduction

Whether you're a naturalist, a naturist, a surfer or a sunbather, there's a beach in Britain that's perfect for *you*. This book celebrates 100 of the very best beaches to be found along the 11,000 miles of Britain's beautiful and varied coastline, from the donkey rides and kiss-me-quick charm of Blackpool's Golden Mile to the hottest surf spots of the South West and the remotest shores of the Isle of Mull.

Today, as much as ever, the appeal of a day at the beach endures. There can be few of us who don't take great pleasure in walking barefoot along spacious sands left immaculate by a receding tide, or who quicken our pace on spotting the sparkling ocean as we climb a belt of golden dunes. Just the sight of a distant watery horizon can have restorative properties for the weary urbanite. For others, it is not the great expanses that are of interest but the miniature worlds of rock pools or the flotsam and jetsam flung up by the tide that hold the greatest fascination. Although the beach is often the perfect place to find solitude and peace, it can also be the ultimate summer social venue where beachboys and babes finally get the chance to show off the results of all that hard work at the gym. For the sporty types, there are apparently endless options for water sports, not to mention beach-based activities such as volleyball and – where space (and the local council) permits – kite buggying. Finally, of course, for most of us the beach is the perfect place to spend a hot summer's day among family and friends. On a sandy beach the kids will play for hours armed only with a bucket and spade while mum and dad take a well-earned rest.

The 100 entries featured in this book were chosen to reflect this variety: some beaches are sensational for surfing or swimming; others are famed for their vibrant atmosphere and excellent facilities; still others may have fine coastal walks nearby with stunning scenic views. All are truly outstanding.

However, when researching Britain's best beaches it quickly became clear that there are far more than 100 great beaches in Britain, and for the sake of simplicity I have not included the beaches of Ireland (which has some truly great beaches and merits a book of its own). Wherever you are, if your favourite beach isn't featured here, or you're adamant that I've missed an absolute belter, please contact me at the address below and I'll try to include it in the next edition.

Stuart Kirby

Contact us at:

studio cactus ltd

13 SOUTHGATE STREET WINCHESTER HAMPSHIRE SO23 9DZ
E-MAIL: MAIL@STUDIOCACTUS.CO.UK

Beaches – awash with history

A sea change

Strange as it may seem, today's beach culture is strongly linked to the discovery of spring water in Scarborough, which is generally regarded as the first British seaside resort. When these health-giving waters were originally found, flowing from a cliff-side spring in 1620, the discovery meant that the town soon joined Bath, Buxton and Harrogate as one of the most elegant places of relaxation and rejuvenation for the wealthiest members of British society. Scarborough remained distinct from its contemporaries, however, in that it was Britain's only coastal spa town. By the 1750s, the health benefits of bathing in (and even drinking) seawater were seen in the same light as the consumption of spring water – and the practice was often heartily endorsed by the local doctor, keen to promote their home town. Scarborough's continued prosperity was assured.

Daring to bare

Along with the 18th-century fashion for sea bathing came the introduction of horse-drawn bathing machines which, by means of an ingenious wheeled tent-and-pulley 'modesty hood', allowed even the most timid to enter the water discreetly without fear of offending others. Bathing machines were popular for a couple of centuries, but as attitudes towards naked flesh relaxed and bathing gradually became a less formal affair, these contraptions slowly became obsolete and began to disappear from Britain's beach resorts.

Bathing machines advertising Beecham's Pills on Bridlington Sands, circa 1900

A new dawn

Following Scarborough's success as a seaside resort, other coastal areas soon developed. Brighton's proximity to London meant that it quickly became a popular place for 'taking the waters'. At the same time, the sleepy fishing village of Blackpool began promoting itself as the coastal resort of choice for the workers of industrial cities in the northwest of England. At the end of the 19th century a rapid growth in seaside holidays occurred. Victorian Britain witnessed a combination of the emergence of a middle class (with time and money to spend), the arrival of train routes from towns and cities to coastal resorts, and the introduction by parliament of bank holidays (in 1871), enabling many families to experience a day on the beach for the first time.

7

The big cover-up: sunscreen protection was just as important in 1918 as it is today

The tide turns

It was only when the First World War started that things began to change for the worse for Britain's seaside resorts. The Second World War exacerbated the problem – with the population's priority being survival, the chances of a summer trip to the seaside were slim.

A holiday epoch of a different kind began in the 1960s with the birth of affordable package deals, meaning that the masses were now heading to Mediterranean beach resorts instead of home-grown destinations. By the 1970s, many of the UK's traditional seaside resorts had become tired and run-down, desperately in need of restoration as beach attractions closed and dilapidated shores were left unkempt.

Beaches are back

So have Britain's beaches been lost for ever? The answer is an emphatic 'no'! Official figures indicate that Britain's bathing water is cleaner than ever. The restoration that goes into our cherished piers, and the hours spent keeping the sands clean and litter free, are evidence that our beaches have a future and not just a glorious past. The tacky image of clapped-out facilities has gone, and better beaches have led to a rise in tourism. More than 30 million people a year are now heading for the British seaside for four nights or more, and some 110 million daytrippers also make for the coast each year. Even the effects of global warming can be viewed through rose-tinted spectacles (in the short term at least): our summers are a couple of degrees hotter. Seldom has there been a better time to plot your route, pack a picnic and head for a day out at one of Britain's many beautiful beaches.

A grand day out

The beach in all its glory

Traditional British seaside resorts have always served one particular purpose – to entertain us. Whether it's the air of childish innocence in playing with buckets and spades to build sandcastles, a fascination with nature (rock pools, starfish, gulls and seaweed), tasty seaside food (think fish and chips, candyfloss, ice cream and rock) or simple, old-fashioned beach activities (anyone for donkey rides, Punch and Judy, and a walk along the pier?), the object of a day out at the beach is to have fun. But have you ever wondered about the origins of these traditions? Where did they come from and why are they still popular today?

A bite to eat

Eating fish and chips at the end of the pier on a beautiful summer's day has to be one of the most magical beach experiences. This quintessentially English meal was first cooked up as the Industrial Revolution gathered pace in the 18th and 19th centuries, and it was in ports around the country that sales really took off. For those with a more 'discerning' palate, sand-and-vinegar-soaked whelks and cockles provide you with a taste of

Victorian seaside Britain. And for dessert? Candy canes, toffee apples, giant lollipops, pick 'n' mix…a day at the seaside is heaven for those with a sweet tooth. The biggest confectionery culprit has to be lettered rock – a luminous pink, peppermint cylinder of hard, boiled sugar about a foot long and an inch in diameter – responsible for thousands of broken crowns and aching molars. First produced in the early 19th century, exactly how rock makers insert the ring of bright red letters remains a mystery to most even today.

Sandcastles

Buckets and spades are thought to have become part of beach life in the mid- to late 19th century. Perhaps the pleasure in building a sandcastle lies in the pure folly of the exercise, as the tide will soon destroy the results of your hard work. Dedicated builders should note that the sand on Weymouth beach is said to be especially good for constructing sandcastles and for sand sculpture. The secret's in the tamping down, apparently.

Piers

The oldest pier in Britain can be found at Ryde, on the Isle of Wight. It was built in 1814. Given the extravagant appearance of many piers, it is surprising to learn that they were originally constructed for the thoroughly practical purpose of allowing ships with goods or tourists to dock safely at parts of the coast that lacked a harbour. Perhaps it is less surprising to learn that pier envy soon developed, and resorts began to strive to have the biggest and best piers in order to attract more tourists. Piers soon became attractions in their own right and offered a place to stroll or enjoy a wide range of entertainment, including side-shows, theatres and gaming machines. Although many piers have now been claimed by the sea, where possible they have been preserved.

Punch and Judy

This celebrated puppet show has thrilled British children for almost 350 years. Punch and Judy booths are as much a part of the stereotypical beach resort scene as donkey rides and deck chairs. Derived from Italian street theatre, this politically incorrect show depicts the brutal and deceitful Punch in bitter relations with his wife, Judy, as well as a policeman, a crocodile, the devil and a crying baby. The hooked-nose Punch usually pummels his enemies, much to the delight of the transfixed children. Despite the controversy, Punch and Judy shows live on in many of Britain's coastal resorts, and there are said to be 300 'professors' practising in the UK.

Donkey rides

A favourite with mothers of hyperactive children, donkey rides are still popular on a handful of Britain's beaches. The sands at Weston-Super-Mare have been home to donkey rides since 1886. So popular is the attraction that a few years ago it fought off the threat of beach helicopter rides – an attempt to pull in tourists with "a vibrant and more attractive attraction", according to a Helicopter Museum spokesman.

Saucy seaside postcards

Fat ladies, henpecked husbands, busty dumb blondes...they've all been depicted in the uniquely British brand that is the traditional seaside postcard. Dating back to the 1880s, these cheeky relics were produced by Yorkshire-based designers Bamforth and Co. At their peak, sales topped 16 million a year. With their risqué slant on life, they celebrated the fun and freedom of seaside holidays. However, as tastes changed, and beach resorts fell out of favour, sales plummeted. The Bamforth and Co. factory closed in 1988, but its hometown of Holmfirth boasts a museum dedicated to its famous postcard manufacturer.

Preserving Britain's coastlines

Thankfully, the most beautiful and unique parts of Britain's coastlines are protected in a variety of ways, and many beaches featured in this guide exist in their current state of splendour as a consequence. A great deal of this geographic triumph is down to the efforts of the National Trust. Since it started in 1965, the National Trust's Neptune Coastline Campaign has been committed to raising funds to help save coastal areas under threat. To date, over 400 miles of coastline have been purchased and preserved. Beaches owned or managed by the National Trust that are featured in this guide include Porthcurno in Cornwall (see page 65), Barafundle Bay in Pembrokeshire (see page 132) and Compton Bay on the Isle of Wight (see page 21).

Another organization that seeks to protect our prime coasts and beaches is the Countryside Agency, by designating them as one or more of the following categories:

Heritage Coasts

Heritage Coasts are spectacular scenic coastlines that are managed to conserve their natural beauty. The first Heritage Coast was the white chalk cliffs of Beachy Head in Sussex. Now about 32 per cent (640 miles) of the coastline of England and 33 per cent (310 miles) of the coastline of Wales is protected.

The stunning Jurassic Coast of Dorset and East Devon is protected as a World Heritage Site as a result of its outstanding geology, which represents 185 million years of earth history. English Nature has numerous National Nature Reserves along the coast, where important areas of plant and animal wildlife habitat are protected. These reserves welcome nature-loving visitors.

National Parks

Representing the most beautiful expanses of countryside in England and Wales, national parks are also home to some of our most important plant and animal species. One of the main purposes of these

The beach at Dorset's Durdle Door makes up just a small part of the Jurassic Coast – 95 miles of spectacular coastline that represents 185 million years of earth history

15

parks is to conserve and enhance natural beauty, wildlife and cultural heritage. Supreme stretches of shoreline lying within national parks can be found in Exmoor, the Lake District (Ravenglass and Silecroft are beaches featured in this book), North York Moors (Robin Hood's Bay, Whitby, Kettleness Sands, Runswick Bay, and Staithes appear within these pages), Pembrokeshire Coast (read on to learn about Saundersfoot, Barafundle Bay, and Whitesand Bay), and Snowdonia (which includes Harlech, another beach featured in this book).

Areas of Outstanding Natural Beauty (AONBs)

The true natural wonders of our landscape, designated AONBs cover about 15 per cent of England and 4 per cent of Wales. The primary purposes of AONBs are to conserve areas of natural beauty that do not have recreational opportunities and protect them outside of the national parks system. The first designated Area of Outstanding Natural Beauty was the Gower Peninsula in South Wales in 1956. Since then, 41 areas in England and Wales have been given AONB status.

Setting the standards at Britain's beaches

There are a number of organizations and schemes in existence that aim to make our time at Britain's beaches as safe and enjoyable as possible. The best known is the Blue Flag scheme, awarded annually in the UK since 1987 by ENCAMS, an environmental campaigns group. The Blue Flag award recognizes the very best in beach management, including health and safety provision, the EC Guideline water quality standard, clean sand, good facilities and good accessibility. This book features 30 Blue Flag award-winning beaches, which are highlighted by the appearance of a blue flag symbol at the bottom of the entry. For the latest information and other details about Blue Flag beaches, visit www.seasideawards.org.uk.

The Seaside Awards scheme also acknowledges Britain's best beaches, but whereas Blue Flag focuses only on resort beaches, the Seaside Awards also include rural beaches. In Wales, the Green Coast Award recognizes beaches in a natural and unspoilt environment with excellent water quality. See www.keepwalestidy.org for further details. For a comprehensive guide to bathing-water quality in the UK, the Marine Conservation Society's guide is available online at www.goodbeachguide.co.uk. Finally, on issues of beach safety, the Marine and Coastguard Agency campaigns hard to reduce the number of preventable accidents at the beach by warning people about issues such as water safety. Visit their website at www.mcga.gov.uk.

Symbols used in this book

⌀	Pebble beach	♦♦	Toilets
⌂	Sandy beach	�	Pub nearby
⌒	Surf beach	⌐	Shops nearby
⌇	Suitable for water sports	🍽	Restaurant or café nearby
Ⓟ	Pay parking (otherwise free parking)	🐕	Dogs welcome all year (no summer ban applies)

This beach has been awarded the Blue Flag for cleanliness

South East England

Avon

Christchurch is located between Bournemouth and Lymington. From Christchurch,
take the A35, heading towards Highcliffe and then Mudeford. The beach is signposted.

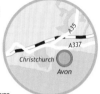

Avon beach is one of Christchurch's most
popular beaches, appealing to families and
water-sports enthusiasts alike. At low tide
small sandbanks are revealed, creating
sheltered lagoons; wading out to find a
private patch of beach is great fun on a warm
summer's day, but do keep an eye out for the incoming tide
or you'll be left high and…wet!

Excellent offshore conditions keep windsurfers happy, and
as the car park is behind the beach, it is only a short distance
to carry equipment. If you're peckish, a beachside café
serves a good selection of snacks and home-made food.

Nearby Hengistbury Head is also definitely worth a visit. Park
at Mudeford Quay and take the short boat ride over to the
natural sandstone headland, lined with hundreds of beach
huts. From here you can enjoy good views of the Isle of Wight.

Swap beaches for the ancient woodlands of the New Forest
National Park by driving inland a few miles along the A35.

Compton Bay

Located on the A3055 coastal road, close to Hanover Point, between
Freshwater and Brook.

Considered by many to be the Isle of Wight's
finest beach, this wide, rural, sandy stretch
on the island's southwest coast forms part
of the Tennyson Heritage Coast and is
managed by the National Trust.

From the clean beach there are striking views of
the white cliffs further along the coast, which peak at 147m
(480ft) at Tennyson Down. This area is reliable for decent

waves – so surfing's a
good option – and
swimming is safe. A
coastal path passes
behind the beach,
and you can enjoy
scenic clifftop walks
in either direction.

**Drive west up the coast a few minutes to Alum Bay for the Isle
of Wight's magnum opus – a grandstand view of the Needles.**

Ryde

Ryde beach is well signposted from the A3055 to the south and the A3054
to the west.

One of the largest town's on the island, Ryde
is a family resort with miles of gently
shelving sand. Facing the Solent, at low tide
the beach is fully exposed, which means a
long walk to the sea but ideal conditions
for an innings or two of beach cricket.

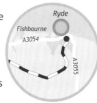

The beach is well managed – with lifeguards, zoned areas,
regularly cleaned sand and plenty of attractions to keep

the family entertained whatever the
weather – but it's not a beach for
those seeking peace and quiet during
summer. Ryde's esplanade features a
marina, gardens and plenty of places
to buy food, drink and a bucket and
spade. Try to visit its Georgian pier too
– the oldest in the UK, built in 1814.

**The Isle of Wight Steam Railway departs from nearby
Smallbrook Junction, snaking westwards to Wootton.**

Sandown

Well signposted from all directions. Follow the A3055 coastal road from the north or south, or the A3056 from inland.

Sandown is one of the Isle of Wight's most popular and traditional resort beaches. Families, particularly with youngsters, are drawn to its beachside play areas and trampolines, a land train and miles of clean, sandy beach. The sea is typically very safe for swimming, with lifeguards on duty during the summer. If it's water sports and not bathing you're into, then you'll

appreciate the opportunities for canoeing, jet-skiing and speedboat rides.

Deck chairs, chalets and other essential kit can be hired, and the beach is machine-cleaned during the summer months.

Seaweed and litter collected from Sandown beach during cleaning are used as compost by local farmers.

23

St Helens

From the A3055 follow signs for St Helens along the B3330. To reach the beach follow the sign to The Duver.

Secluded, peaceful, sand-and-shingle St Helens beach lies on the Isle of Wight's rural east coast, backed by the remains of St Helens church. Next to the beach is The Duver, an area of National Trust-owned grassland and sand dunes – an ideal spot for picnicking. Behind the sea wall is the licensed Baywatch On The Beach café, selling hot and cold food, ice creams and all sorts of beach goods. The beach is excellent for swimming and rock pooling, and

at the far end you'll find a small, rocky headland known as Nodes Point – also National Trust. Litter-picked daily in the summer, the coast here is unusual in that many of the beach huts are made from old, converted railway carriages.

A walk southwards to Bembridge's busy little harbour is highly recommended. Watch the boats sail to and fro as you lunch.

West Wittering

From the A27 take the A286, signposted 'The Witterings', and follow signs for West Wittering beach.

Everybody has a favourite beach…and for many people West Wittering is that very beach. Its popularity and close proximity to London mean that it can get very busy during the summer. However, the area's beautiful natural surroundings make it an equally enjoyable place to visit all year round.

The beach is vast, sandy and gently shelving. At low tide, water collects in pockets, creating the perfect natural paddling pools for kids. There are also over 150 beach huts, all privately owned, for which demand is huge.

An added bonus is that the coast here is always kept in pristine condition by its owners, the West Wittering Preservation Trust.

Bordering the western end of the beach is East Head, a spit which is a Site of Special Scientific Interest (SSSI).

Littlehampton

Well signposted from the A27. The A259 also leads to Littlehampton from both the east and west.

This is a very large shingle beach that exposes a multitude of sandy spots at low tide – definitely a popular place for a relaxing day or two of fun in the sun. Littlehampton beach is prime family territory due to its spaciousness, good amenities and

the lifeguards who look out from their tower during the summer. First-aid and lost-child facilities are also big factors.

Walk along the beach after stormy weather and you'll be amazed at the treasure trove left in its wake: crabs, sponges, cuttlefish bones, whelk egg

West Sussex has an embarrassment of riches: the sumptuous South Downs are a short drive inland, as is

26

cases that look like bubble wrap...the kids will love it. Look inland and you'll see that the shoreline is backed by a stretch of brightly coloured huts, gleaming in the sunlight like daytime lighthouses.

Further down the beach is a children's play area, but if you really want to treat them, then a trip to Harbour Park entertainment centre is in order: slides, rides, trampolines, arcades and mini golf – it even has a climbing wall. And for mum and dad? Littlehampton's nautically-themed shopping centre offers traditional high street stores with a variety of interesting, independent shops and markets. And you won't go hungry – there's a good selection of eateries serving fresh seafood, fish and chips, pub grub, light snacks and international cuisine.

Arundel, with its 11th-century castle. Or drive westwards to the Roman city of Chichester and take in the cathedral and harbour.

Brighton

Well signposted from the A27 to the east and west, and from the A23 to the north.
Follow signs for the seafront.

Whether you want fish and chips and an ice cream on the beach, or fine dining and hip hotels, Brighton will not disappoint. It is one of Britain's oldest seaside resorts but continues to evolve, making it an exciting place to visit. It is also one of Britain's newest cities – achieving its city status in 2000.

Brighton's seafront seems to offer everything for an active

day by the sea: walking, swimming, basketball, volleyball, kayaking, surfing, cycling, rollerblading – the list goes on. For younger visitors there is a children's play area, paddling pool and carousel rides. If you'd rather ride the coast than walk it, take the Volk's Electric

Brighton's Royal Pavilion started life as just a Sussex farmhouse by the sea, but for the last 300 years it has grown into a haven of

Railway – England's oldest – along Madeira Drive to the marina, admiring the fine Regency terraces as you go. East of the main city area and next to Peter Pan's playground, Brighton also has a clearly marked nudist beach.

Away from the beach there are a wealth of places to eat, drink and party. In addition to great bars and clubs there are over 400 restaurants to choose from. Brighton's dramatic architecture only adds to its attraction, with Regency seafront squares and crescents framing the city's two piers. Brighton Pier was opened in 1899 and still offers traditional seaside amusements, such as fairground attractions, side stalls and candyfloss. West Pier, however, remains badly damaged following fierce storms in the 1970s and fires in recent years.

opulence and eccentricity. Don't leave without witnessing its Indian-style domes – think the Taj Mahal – and Chinese-style interior.

Seaford

Use the A26 from the north or the A259 from the east and west. Follow the signs to Seaford Bay.

The first thing to catch your eye is the dramatic white chalk cliff face of Seaford Head. Located approximately halfway between Brighton and Eastbourne, this is an extensive pebble beach that is typical of the area. It is relatively undeveloped but is far from rural.

Particularly popular with families today, the arrival of the railway in 1864 saw Seaford begin to blossom as a favourite Victorian and Edwardian seaside resort.

Standing proud on the seafront is a Martello tower, built

at the turn of the 19th century as a Napoleonic defence. Restored to near-original condition, the tower is now home to the Seaford Local History Museum – go and explore its 5,000 square feet of yesteryear.

If Seaford Head doesn't amaze you, then the nearby coastline of Seven Sisters and Beachy Head are guaranteed to.

Eastbourne

Well signposted from the A27, join either the A22 or A2270. From the A259 simply follow the road south.

Eastbourne is one of Britain's most famous beach resorts, renowned for having the best sunshine record in the country. It's a shingle beach, but sandy stretches magically appear at mid to low tide. Beach huts, sun loungers and umbrellas can be hired, and lifeguards are on hand throughout the summer months.

Five miles of promenade stretch along the shore, from Sovereign Harbour in the east to the majestic 150m (500ft) high cliffs of Beachy Head in the west – the

highest chalk sea cliff in Britain. You should also wander past the stunning Carpet Gardens, the 1930s bandstand, several Martello towers and the sympathetically restored Victorian pier.

Eastbourne is the location for the annual premier pre-Wimbledon ladies' tennis tournament.

Norman's Bay

From the west, take the minor road from the A27/A259 roundabout. This narrow lane leads you to the beach.

This pebble-cum-shingle beach lies between Eastbourne and Hastings. If you don't fancy driving to Norman's Bay, this rural spot is unusual in that its own train station is located directly behind the beach. Regular services operate to Eastbourne, Lewes and London.

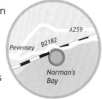

The relative isolation of Norman's Bay means you can have the beach (almost) to yourself most of the year round. Facilities are fairly basic: designated areas for water sports are provided, and there's a camping/caravanning site nearby.

If you're wondering about the significance of the name, William the Conqueror is said to have landed here before the Battle of Hastings in 1066.

Follow the coast eastwards to Bexhill-on-Sea and visit the De La Warr Pavilion, a stunning Grade I listed building.

Camber Sands

Signposted from the A259 in both directions, east and west. Follow the coast road to Camber.

Camber Sands is everything you would hope a British beach to be: a huge swathe of soft, golden sand, bordered by magnificent dunes. The beach is also very well managed, making it a safe and relaxing place to spend the day – I'd say it's an ideal family venue.

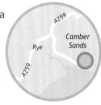

Low tide reveals glorious stretches of unbroken sand, perfect for beach cricket, sandcastle construction and kite

flying; not so great for swimmers and paddlers who hate long walks! The beach is zoned: windsurfers and kite flyers are restricted to a section between the Western car park and Rye harbour, and dog walkers also have designated areas of beach between May and September.

Just a 10-minute drive from Camber, perched on the hillside, is the medieval Cinque Port town of Rye.

St Margaret's Bay

Follow signs for St Margaret's at Cliffe from the A258. Drive through the village and on to the bay.

Located between Deal and Dover, St Margaret's Bay lies at the narrowest point of the Strait of Dover, where England and France are just 21 miles apart.

The bay is fairly small and the shingle beach is backed by chalk cliffs. There is a steep descent

to the beach, so tread carefully. At low tide, rock pools are ripe for exploring by kids of all ages! Facilities are fairly basic, but you'll find The Coastguard bar and restaurant behind the beach for a refuel. Well worth visiting is South Foreland Lighthouse, a Victorian construction built on top of the cliffs to steer ships clear of the treacherous Goodwin Sands, otherwise known as 'the ship swallower'.

St Margaret's Bay has, at different times, been home to Lord Byron, Noel Coward, Ian Fleming and Peter Ustinov.

Joss Bay

Take the B2052 coastal road from Broadstairs or Margate. The beach is signposted from here.

Created naturally by a large expanse of sand backed by cliffs, Joss Bay forms an inviting, rustic setting. It attracts families – bathing is good – but it is Kent's surfing fraternity who are the biggest Joss Bay fans; the long, shallow crescent provides ideal conditions for water sports. A snack shop, first-aid post, lost-child centre and lifeguard patrols in the summer ensure everyone is catered for.

If it's walking you're into, then join the Viking Coastal Trail here. This scenic 28-mile circular walk takes in the whole of the Thanet coastline before looping back through Kent's villages. Joss Bay is a short distance along the coast from the seaside resort of Margate, which offers a good selection of shops, bars and restaurants – all particularly handy given Joss Bay's out-of-the-way location. Alternatively, head south to Ramsgate.

No longer an island, many centuries ago the Isle of Thanet was divided from the mainland by the Wantsum Channel.

Kingsgate Bay

From Margate, take the A255 before turning left on to B2052. From Ramsgate, follow the coastal road north.

After rounding a bend in the coastal road, the sight of Kingsgate Bay is an unforgettable one: the beach is enclosed by white chalk cliffs that have a natural arch (as pictured) at the far end. Overlooking the whole landscape is the imperious Kingsgate Castle.

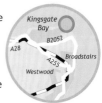

The cliffs and other seafront areas here are supposedly riddled with caves and tunnels once used by pirates, so it wasn't a great surprise to learn of the aptly named Smugglers' Cave, situated behind The Captain Digby family pub and restaurant.

The beach is fairly isolated, with few facilities, but it's perfect for summer bathing or for bracing winter walks as the winds whip in from the Channel.

Charles Dickens fans take note – Broadstairs is home to The Dickens House Museum. The Dickens Festival is held in June.

Tankerton

From the M2, follow the signs to Whitstable on the A299 and then the A290.
Then follow local signs to Tankerton.

Situated approximately one mile east of
Whitstable town centre, this lovely stretch of
timber-groyned shingle beach is backed
by the grassed lawns of Marine Parade. It is
from this promenade that you'll get the best
view of 'the street', a long shingle strand that
appears about half a mile out at low tide. A row of colourful
beach huts also provides Tankerton with a little character.

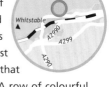

The beach here is less well known than its big brother
counterpart of Whitstable, but don't
let this put you off. You can still buy
ice creams and snacks from the small
shop behind the beach, and the
licensed Marine Hotel serves larger
meals or drinks in the lounge – a great
spot to sit and watch the waves.

A short drive inland from Whitstable is the historic city of
Canterbury, with its famous 6th-century cathedral.

Whitstable

Follow M2, then A299 and A290 to Whitstable. Then follow the local signs to the seafront. The nearest train station is Whitstable.

Whitstable has evolved into the perfect small seaside town. Whatever the weather, there is plenty on offer to keep visitors entertained for the day. Seafront attractions include yachting, water skiing, boating, fishing and swimming. The area has also established itself as a popular weekend-break destination for those just in search of a little relaxation and fresh air.

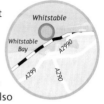

The attractive shingle and pebble beach is divided by Whitstable harbour, which opened in 1832 and was the

first to be served by a railway. The venue of daily catches of fresh oysters, cockles, mussels, whelks and prawns, vendors sell their fare from here and on the beach, should you wish to sample it. Once sated, I

Don't miss the annual Whitstable Oyster Festival, a week-long celebration held in July. It's the perfect excuse to enjoy a few oysters

think the groyned beach to the west of the harbour is the best place to settle down for the day, as the town's attractions and facilities are close to hand.

The beach aside, a major part of the town's charm lies in its numerous lanes and alleys (look out for Squeeze Gut Alley!), lined with pretty weather-boarded cottages, rows of brightly coloured beach huts and enticing shopping streets. Not unusually for a seaside resort, Whitstable is also famous for its beautiful sunsets – well worth waiting for.

The most interesting shops in Whitstable are along Harbour Street, with quality craft shops and places selling contemporary art by local artists. Foodies can choose from a delicatessen, traditional teashop and fish and chip shop. Seafood restaurants abound in the region – Whitstable Oyster Fishery Co., (pictured above), is one of the best. Alternatively, the fish market in the harbour will always sell you something tasty to take home.

with a glass of champagne and then witness pearl diving, go crabbing, take a ghost tour and enjoy the Whitstable Carnival.

Southend-on-Sea, Shoeburyness

There is good access to Southend-on-Sea from the M25 along the A13 or A127, or along the A130 from Chelmsford. Beaches are signposted.

Close to the capital yet still an authentic seaside resort, Southend-on-Sea's claim to fame is that it is home to the world's longest pleasure pier, which extends for over a mile into the Thames Estuary.

Southend has seven miles of spectacular seafront, from Blue Flag holder Shoeburyness (one of my top 100 beaches) in the west to Leigh-on-Sea in the east. Three Shells beach, close to the pier, is a sandy family favourite. Jubilee beach offers the cafés and shops of Marine Parade. And the tiny Bell Wharf beach is famous for its cockles. Kite surfers should head to the designated areas of Shoeburyness East beach.

Southend-on-Sea is twinned with Sopot, a similarly sunny stretch lying on Poland's Baltic coast.

Frinton-on-Sea

From Colchester to the west, follow the A113 then take the B1033 following signs to Frinton. The beach is easily accessible off the main street of Connaught Avenue.

Frinton-on-Sea boasts an uncommercialized and peaceful beach that offers little besides the simple pleasures of cliffs, sand and sea – something the townspeople pride themselves on. There isn't a great deal of beach at high tide, but the shore becomes a hive of activity when the waves recede: safe bathing and clean water mean traditional family fun is the order of the day.

A short walk away, Connaught Avenue offers a fine selection of shops and eateries. Until 2000, however, Frinton had the unusual claim to fame of being a seaside resort without a pub. Despite fierce opposition, the Lock & Barrel finally opened its doors in time for the new millennium.

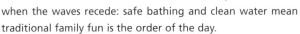

Manningtree, 10 miles northwest of Frinton, is reputed to be Britain's smallest market town. Take a minute to walk round it.

Aldeburgh

Located between Ipswich and Southwold. Take the A1094 from the main
A12 road and follow the signs.

With its long, mainly shingle beach and the
seductive scenery of the Suffolk Heritage
Coast, Aldeburgh is a great place to
recharge your batteries. Just ask the painters
and photographers who frequent it. The
beach is backed by a broad promenade and a
row of elegant houses, creating an essentially urban setting
that has a chilled, laid-back feel.

Aldeburgh is still an active fishing
town, and you can buy the freshest
seafood imaginable from the
boats that pull up to the shore.
Afterwards, take the opportunity to
view lifeboats close-up at the Royal
National Lifeboat Station, home
to these heroic vessels since 1851.

Created in the 1940s by the composer Benjamin Britten, the
Aldeburgh Festival of Music takes place every June.

Southwold

From the main A12 road follow either the A1095 from the south or B1127 from the north to Southwold. The main car park is located next to the pier.

Southwold has a reputation for being a beach destination with a slight air of superiority and old-world charm. Look no further than its Victorian pier – first built in 1899, after falling into disrepair a local businessman renovated it in 2002 to Pier of the Year standard.

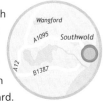

Now it has its own bar, restaurant and café, as well as amusements and a viewing telescope – to spot pirates with. On the beach there is a special area reserved for water sports, which include water skiing and windsurfing. Fishing, with a permit, is allowed off the pier. For children there's a boating lake, model yacht pond, and Punch and Judy shows in summer. For dad there's a pint of locally brewed Adnams beer.

Southwold's modest-looking beach huts can fetch rather immodest prices – one went for £45,000 in 2003.

Lowestoft

Located south of Great Yarmouth, Lowestoft is easily reached from the coastal A12 road or the A146 from inland.

Lowestoft's motto, *'Point du Jour'*, means break of day. Being the most easterly town in Britain, its sandy beaches catch the sun's rays first every morning. Bordered by the exquisite beauty of the nearby Broads, the main beach is a sandy, lively resort with two piers: South Pier and Claremont Pier.

The region retains the feel of a well-maintained and welcoming family resort. In the summer it caters admirably for children,

with sandcastle competitions, trampolining and an adventure play area – all under the gaze of trained lifeguards. Beach huts and chalets are available for hire too, adding a touch of charm from days gone by.

 Situated next to the seafront are Sparrow's Nest gardens, housing the Lowestoft Maritime Museum.

Great Yarmouth

Great Yarmouth is located east of Norwich. It is well signposted and is accessible along the A47 from inland.

Along with the likes of Blackpool and Scarborough, Great Yarmouth is a classic example of a traditional British seaside resort. Showing its age in places, it still has over 15 miles of glorious sandy beaches and enough attractions to keep the whole family entertained. And fun is what Great Yarmouth's all about. During summer the main stretch of beach gets very busy due to, among other events, organized beach soccer and volleyball, but you can always discover your own nook and cranny if you crave quiet. Step off the sand and there are plenty of ways to spend what's left of the kids' pocket money: the golden mile boasts the Pleasure Beach, with its trampolines, adventure playgrounds, roller coasters, karting and more. For mum and dad, nightlife is just as comprehensive and includes a raft of restaurants, bars, nightclubs, cinemas, theatres and casinos.

Take a boat trip from the beach to Scroby Sands, where you can come face to face with seals.

45

Wells-next-the-Sea

Wells-next-the-Sea is fairly remote but is easily accessible along Norfolk's A149 coastal road.

Despite not actually being next to the sea, Norfolk's Wells-next-the-Sea still qualifies as a lovely little coastal resort. Visitors take a mini shuttle train that runs along the sea wall from the quaint town across the salt marshes to the part-pebble, part-sand beach.

Here, you feel a real sense of being in the countryside, but

surrounded by brightly coloured beach huts on stilts and the odd moored boat. At low tide the beach reveals countless rock pools as well as a seemingly infinite amount of space for beach games, kite flying and walking. The town itself continues to be a working port, with cobbled streets, tea rooms and antique shops.

Twenty miles away is Sandringham House, the Queen's country retreat, which offers a fascinating insight into royal life.

Holkham

Access to the pay car park is directly from the A149 coastal road to the west of Wells-next-the-Sea.

Holkham's beach is the perfect escape for those who love wide open spaces and lungs full of fresh sea air. The clean, sandy beach is backed by pine woodlands, and at low tide the sea can be so far out it almost appears to be on the horizon. Entrance to the

beach car park isn't well signposted – keep an eye out along the coastal road for signs to Holkham Hall.

The sheer size of this beach makes it popular with all types of people, from walkers to kite flyers to naturists to naturalists;

the naturalists are drawn to Holkham National Nature Reserve, and the naturists to the official naturist beach, which is located about a mile west along the beach.

Holkham beach achieved star status when Gwyneth Paltrow appeared on it during the filming of *Shakespeare in Love*.

Hunstanton

Leaving the roundabout where the A148 and A149 meet, Hunstanton is well signposted along the A149 coastal road.

Unique in that it is the UK's only east coast holiday resort that faces west, this isn't the sole quality that makes Hunstanton stand out. This Norfolk region offers classic family attractions on its mainly sandy beach backed by towering chalk cliffs, including a funfair, pony rides, sea life sanctuary and the Princess Theatre.

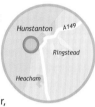

The seawater here is very calm and safe for bathing. In fact, it is these mirror-calm conditions that make Hunstanton an ideal destination for many popular water sports, including water skiing, windsurfing, sailing, kite surfing and jet skiing. The beach does not have lifeguards as such, but 'resort services staff'

Just outside of Hunstanton, on the A149 towards King's Lynn, is Norfolk Lavender – a farm that harvests the distinctive mauve

48

who are first-aid trained and keep beach users safe and happy from Easter until the end of the school holidays in September. A short distance along the coast is Old Hunstanton, a charming village that comprises a medieval church, a smattering of carrstone houses and, more importantly, a beach. The coast here is a popular place for walking man's best friend, since dogs are banned from Hunstanton's main beach. Old Hunstanton also offers access to the nature reserves and coastal footpaths, affording good birdwatching opportunities. Standing a few yards from the beach is a former lighthouse that has been converted in to a hotel – if you do book a room there, best not to ask for one in the light tower!

flower. This Norfolk landmark has operated since the 19th century, and produces over 100 different lavenders to see and smell.

South West England

Bournemouth

Follow signs for Bournemouth from the A35 or A338. Beaches are well signposted. There is also a land train that runs along the promenade and links the beaches.

Bournemouth

On a warm summer's day you could be one of up to more than 100,000 people enjoying Bournemouth's seven miles of beach. Everybody's catered for – for example, there are smoke-free, glass-free and dog-free stretches of coast. These beaches were also the first to introduce the Kidzone scheme where children wear coloured wristbands to prevent them going astray. The scheme operates on eight of Bournemouth's beaches, including

the hugely popular Blue Flag holder Alum Chime. Deckchairs and windbreaks can be hired here, and the water is typically safe for swimming, with lifeguards patrolling during summer.

The Bournemouth Live! festival is held in June, showcasing the best live bands of every genre.

Sandbanks

The main roads leading to Poole are the A35, A350 and A338. The beach is well signposted from the centre of Poole.

Welcome to the Costa del Dorset. Sandbanks is consistently judged to have Britain's best beach, and when the sun shines here you couldn't disagree. Located at the mouth of Poole Harbour, for over 100 years the use of groynes has been required to prevent Sandbanks peninsula and the beach from being washed away altogether – so thank heavens for groynes!

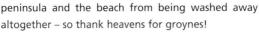

Fine golden sands slope gently to the sea, and careful zoning measures ensure that swimmers, dogs and their owners, and

water-sports enthusiasts all have a part of the beach to themselves. The lifeguard-observed water is gorgeous for swimming, and deckchairs and sunbeds are for hire.

The adjacent beach at Shell Bay lies just across Poole Harbour. It can be reached by car-and-passenger ferry.

53

Studland Bay

From Wareham, follow the A351 in the direction of Swanage then take the B3351, which is signposted to Studland.

Not your typical bucket-and-spade affair, the heathland behind Studland beach is a National Nature Reserve – a haven for many rare birds and other forms of wildlife. This stunning area is protected from the prevailing winds and storms by Old Harry Rocks, the chalk headland that separates Studland from Swanage Bay.

South beach, Middle beach, Knoll beach (with its National

Trust tourist centre) and Shell Bay (which includes a naturist beach) make up three miles of the coastline. Designated zones for swimming and water sports can be found at South beach and Knoll beach. There are no lifeguards, but first-aid trained beach wardens are on duty in the summer.

Studland's beaches can also be reached from Poole and Bournemouth by taking a short ferry crossing from Sandbanks.

Lulworth Cove

Lulworth Cove is clearly signposted from the A352 between Dorchester and Wareham.
Leave the A352 at Wool and head south along the B3071.

A near-perfect semi circle in shape, Lulworth Cove has been carved out of the cliffs by the sea's brute power. The spectacular geology of this area has led to it being designated as a Natural World Heritage Site.

The walk to the cove is lined with numerous shops and cafés selling everything from ice cream and snacks to freshly caught local fish.

Arriving at the shore, you'll find a sheltered shingle beach that provides safe bathing. Be sure to take the 1.5-mile walk along the cliffs to the equally impressive Durdle Door (pictured), a natural 12m (40ft) arch of limestone rock that overlooks a small beach that can be reached by descending the (very steep) steps provided.

Situated in nearby East Lulworth, 17th-century Lulworth Castle and Park welcomes visitors year-round.

Ringstead Bay

From the A353 follow signs through the village of Upton to Ringstead Bay. Only a small wooden sign directs you to the beach, so keep your eyes peeled.

As if being kept a Dorset secret, you reach Ringstead Bay along a narrow country lane that leads down a private road. The beach is a picturesque 65m (210ft) crescent of pebbles with clean water that's safe for bathing. This tranquil spot is perfect for those looking to escape the busier beaches of the surrounding area. Given its remote location, the beach has good facilities. Next

to the large car park is a well-stocked shop selling everything you need for a day at the beach, which doubles as a café selling hot and cold food, including ice creams. The cliffs behind the beach are an excellent place to find fossils, as is typical along this stretch of the coast. The beach shop also sells fossils should you fail to find your own!

Due to their high oil content, the nearby Burning Cliffs have been known to spontaneously combust deep within the rocks.

Weymouth

Follow the A354 south from Dorchester. Weymouth beach and its car parks are signposted. The A353 runs along the sea wall.

King George III gave wonderful Weymouth his royal approval over 200 years ago, and the fine Georgian architecture lining much of the promenade today is testament to his fondness for the region.

The sand on Weymouth's long arc of sand-and-shingle beach is renowned for its particular suitability to sculpture, and you can often see these ephemeral works of art being crafted on the beach. The main bay is a designated bathing area, and zoned areas for water sports are provided

nearby. RNLI lifeguards survey the beach, safety boats patrol the water, and a lost-children and first-aid point ensure safety is a priority here.

If you're looking for a little private sanctuary, drive south to the Isle of Portland – Church Ope Cove is an absolute gem.

Branscombe

Branscombe is located between Exeter and Lyme Regis, and is signposted from the A3052.

Situated on the East Devon Heritage Coast – also known as the Jurassic Coast because of its prehistoric connections – Branscombe proffers a beautifully maintained beach in an irresistibly natural setting. You'll find it at the end of a long, winding country lane that passes through the village of Branscombe, with its pubs and National Trust properties: the Old Bakery, Manor Mill and forge.

The shingle beach is a superb place to relax and enjoy the surrounding coastal scenery. There are surprisingly good facilities at Branscombe, with toilets and a car park located close

If unrivalled countryside views are what you're after then head to nearby Seaton and take a tramway ride. The three-mile route runs

to the beach, as well as a small picnic area. There is also a comprehensively stocked shop that sells the most irresistible dairy ice cream. Next to the shop is the Sea Shanty restaurant, which is open every day until 5pm during the summer.

Although I recommend taking a dip in the sea at Branscombe, it's the coastal footpaths sprouting from the beach that really influenced my day there. The walk from Branscombe to Beer – four miles there and back – will wow you with its sensational sea views (be prepared to scale some great heights!), brushes with geological features and ventures through lush vegetation. You'll need a degree of fitness to complete it though!

through East Devon's glorious Axe Valley to Colyton (via Colyford) and lasts 25 minutes from end to end.

Dawlish Warren

From most parts of the country take the M5 towards Exeter, then join the A379. Dawlish Warren is about seven miles from Exeter and is well signposted.

If you love the classic British family seaside experience, this is the place for you. Once you've hired your deckchair from the promenade, you can simply relax on the beach and enjoy fish and chips, followed by a snooze before waking up to an ice cream.

The beach at Dawlish Warren offers plenty of sand (with dunes), safe bathing conditions, and lifeguards who patrol daily throughout summer. There are also specified dog-free and dog-friendly areas. Away from the shore are amusements, rides and a go-kart track for the children, along with numerous gift shops and places to eat.

If you'd rather stretch your legs than sunbathe, then head to the Dawlish Warren National Nature Reserve – nearly 600 different types of flowering plants have been recorded here, including the Warren Crocus (indigenous only to this area).

Dartmoor National Park and its bewitching landscapes are less than half an hour's drive away.

Blackpool Sands

Follow the A379 from Dartmouth. Blackpool Sands is located between
Stoke Fleming and Strete.

Being privately owned, you can guarantee that on any given day Blackpool Sands will stand up to inspection. Its spotless beach consists of fine pebbles, but fear not – there is a sandy area close to the car park exclusively for sandcastle construction! There is

also a freshwater paddling pool, which is perfect for younger children to cool down in on a hot summer's day. For seafarers,

a safe swimming area is marked by a buoyed zone. There's also a lifeguard depot that doubles as a lost-child collection point.

A beach shop, water-sports centre and a pleasant café, serving a wide selection of hot and cold snacks, complete this delightful venue.

Blackpool Sands beach has its own website: check out
www.blackpool-sands.co.uk before you pay a visit.

Slapton Sands

The beach is signposted from the A379, which runs along the coast between
Torcross and Slapton.

Slapton Sands isn't a sandy beach as the name
suggests, but an attractive three-mile stretch
of fine red pebbles and shingle in Start
Bay, south of Dartmouth. The high cliffs,
open fields and dense woodland make this
a very satisfying stretch of seafront.

A shingle ridge dominates the beach here, dividing the sea from
Slapton Ley, a 1.5-mile long freshwater lake. Both a Site of

Special Scientific Interest and a National
Nature Reserve, make the most of this
wildlife haven as it may not be here for
long...the shingle bar protecting it is
being eaten away by the sea. Not in
danger of disappearing soon is the South
West Coast Path, which passes along Start
Bay and includes a number of cycleways.

More than 700 soldiers and sailors died at Slapton Sands in 1944
when the D-Day landing exercise Operation Tiger went wrong.

Bigbury-on-Sea

From the A379, follow the B3392 to Bigbury-on-Sea and then signs to the beach and car park.

Overlooking Burgh Island some 200m (650ft) offshore, Bigbury-on-Sea has a beautiful beach with soft golden sand and a little shingle. It is backed by low cliffs, and on one side lies the River Avon estuary. During summer a passenger ferry service links the region with Bantham on the other side of the estuary. Bigbury-on-Sea is effectively a sand spit, which extends from

the mainland, and at high tide a sea tractor carries visitors over to the island. At low tide you can walk it before rewarding yourself with a drink at the Pilchard Inn, but it's the Art Deco-themed Burgh Island Hotel that's the most talked about landmark on this 10ha (26-acre) beauty spot.

If you're into diving, then the shipwrecks off Bigbury Bay will keep you busy. Set sail from nearby Hope Cove.

Saunton Sands

From Barnstaple, follow the A361, then take the B3231 coastal road. The beach and car park are signposted.

Approaching Saunton Sands along the coast road from Croyde Bay to the north, the sight of the beach stretching to the horizon on a clear day is truly spectacular. The sandy shore is almost three miles long, and when the summer sun shines you're hard-pressed to find a free spot. The solution? Just walk a little further.

The beach is a safe family affair: a lifeguard is on duty in the summer and the water is fine for swimming. Saunton Sands also has good surfing conditions, which are particularly suited

to beginners. The seashore is backed by the beautiful setting of Braunton Burrows, a collection of sand dunes that have been classified as a biosphere reserve by UNESCO.

South of Saunton is the Taw–Torridge estuary. The River Taw was made famous in Henry Williamson's *Tarka the Otter*.

Croyde Bay

A short drive along the B3231 from Braunton. The beach is well signposted from the village.

Croyde is blessed with a fantastic beach that lies between the headlands of Baggy Point to the north and Saunton Down to the south. It has some of the best conditions for surfing in the whole of the South West. There are three main surfing areas – Croyde Reef at the northern end of

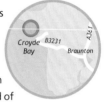

Croyde Bay, Croyde Beach and Downend Point – and the waves become very crowded in summer. The actual beach comprises sand, huge dunes and some rocks, and there are excellent walks

along the surrounding cliffs. Croyde's delightful village also offers a range of pubs, shops and restaurants, as well as surf shops hiring out equipment and a range of gear for other water sports.

Check out the surf conditions at Croyde Bay by viewing the webcam at www.croyde-surf-cam.com.

Woolacombe Bay

Follow the B3343 to Woolacombe, which is accessible from the A361 from Braunton or the A3123 from the east.

Located between Ilfracombe and Braunton, Woolacombe is equipped to offer the perfect experience for all types of beach lover. Whether it's fine walks, golden sands or a top surf spot you're after, Woolacombe delivers.

The coast consists of over two miles of clean sandy beach sheltered by the headlands of Baggy and Morte Points. It is a beach that appeals to families, as the water is safe for swimming and patrolled by lifeguards in summer.

Atlantic Ocean waves make this one of the most popular

surf beaches in the area, and ramblers will love the South West Coast Path National Trail or the Tarka Trail, which takes in the Exmoor National Park.

Nearby Barricane Beach is famous for its exotic shells, carried across the Atlantic Ocean by the Gulf Stream.

Combe Martin

Leave the A361 just past South Molton and join the A339. Then follow signs
for Combe Martin along the A399.

Combe Martin, just east of Ilfracombe, lies in an
Area of Outstanding Natural Beauty on the
dramatic north Devon coastline bordering
Exmoor National Park. The village has a long
history of local lead and silver mining.

The attractive beach is a mixture of sand and
pebbles at high tide, revealing plenty of firm, clean sand at
low tide. However, it is the plentiful rock pools that are the
real highlight of this beach, inviting you to delve in and forage.

The beach is also very popular
with water-sports enthusiasts
and is a safe place to swim,
but this is not a beach for
surfers. For serious walkers,
the scenic 13-mile coastal path
east to Lynton is a real beauty.

The Pack of Cards Inn is said to have been built by a local man
celebrating the winnings of a particularly good hand.

Kynance Cove

Leave the A394 at Helston and follow signs for Lizard Point along the A3083.

Then look out for signs to Kynance Cove.

White sands, turquoise waters, serpentine rock faces and towering cliffs make remote Kynance Cove one of Cornwall's most prized beaches. Close to Lizard, the most southerly point of mainland Britain, the vista from these National Trust-protected clifftops is jaw-dropping.

The beach of soft sand is a short walk along the cliffs and down some fairly steep steps. In addition to the natural

beauty here, the man-made aspects are aesthetically pleasing too. Carefully restored historic buildings house the Kynance Café, and their turf-roofed toilets and solar-power slating provide a real sense of coastal self-sufficiency.

Lizard gets its name not from a mythical dragon as some attest, but from the Cornish *lezou*, meaning headland or high place.

Porthcurno

Passing by Penzance, from the A30 Porthcurno can be reached from either the B3315 or B3283.

Porthcurno beach is set in an idyllic, secluded cove, which is located southeast of Land's End. Sheltered by dramatic granite rock formations, the beach and surroundings are managed by the National Trust. The golden-white sands here are said to get their colour from finely crushed seashells, and it's these shells that also give the striking turquoise waters their glorious hue – you'll want to jump in whatever the time of year!

Not far from the beach is the Porthcurno Telegraph Museum.

This fascinating attraction tells the story of how, from 1870, pioneering technology was used to lay undersea telegraph cables from Porthcurno to the far reaches of the British Empire.

The open-air Minack Theatre sits on Porthcurno's coastline, with spectacular views of the Atlantic Ocean as its backdrop.

Sennen Cove

Sennen is well signposted from the A30. Follow the winding, rural roads down to the beach.

The popularity of Sennen Cove in the far west of Cornwall is well deserved – it is a really lovely sandy beach, with clear blue seas and beckoning rural environs. It may be sheltered by the headland of Pedn-men-du, but the winds and accompanying waves of

this west-facing cove still attract hoards of surfers. Sennen Lifeboat Station is a reminder of how powerful the seas can be. However, a safe swimming option can be found

in the natural breakwater between the towering Cape Cornwall and Brison Rocks. There are plenty of places to grab a bite to eat, and you should try to hang around for the stunning sunsets.

For those who prefer walks to waves, follow the path along the cliffs from Sennen Cove to Land's End.

St Ives, Porthmeor Beach

St Ives is signposted from the main A30 road. The beaches are signposted from the town centre.

St Ives is a heavenly seaside town, with its quaint cobbled streets, hidden alleys, proud fishing heritage and, of course, its terrific beaches. One of my top 100, Blue Flag holder Porthmeor is the town's surfing hot spot, but its beautifully clear turquoise waters also attract families. Facilities are good, with parking nearby and lifeguards on duty during the summer.

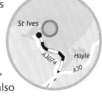

Porthmeor beach

Nearby Porthminster beach, another Blue Flag holder, has a backdrop of palm trees and sub-tropical shrubs, while Porthgwidden and Harbour beaches are more secluded affairs. Inland, St Ives offers plenty of decent shopping, restaurants and cultural attractions, such as the Tate St Ives gallery.

A 30-minute boat trip takes you round the coast to Seal Island where you may spot Atlantic Grey Seals.

Fistral

Follow the A392 from the A30 or A39 main roads. Fistral Beach is signposted from the town centre.

One of Newquay's biggest beaches, Fistral is world famous for the many national and international surfing championships it hosts. Flanked by the Towan and Pentire headlands, the waves here are consistently spectacular, so be careful if it's just a swim you're after. For those new to surfing, the British

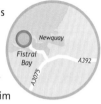

Surfing Association offers lessons from its centre based on the beach. Almost a mile long, Fistral is afforded a little cover from the elements by steep sand dunes and grassland. If it's too blustery for you, though, head to the seclusion of the beach café and bar or the comfortable surroundings of

The days of driving 285 miles over five-and-a-half hours from London to Newquay are no more. Flights now operate between Gatwick and

the lounge of the Headland Hotel and watch the waves crash at the windows as you relax with a drink and a bite to eat.

In the summer, when crowds flock to the area en masse, the limited beach parking can be a nightmare so I strongly advise using the nearby town car parks and then walking to the beach. It isn't far, and by taking a wander you'll encounter the meandering coastal path that runs behind Fistral.

Downtown Newquay has dozens of places to eat, drink and shop. There are also many B&Bs that cater specifically for surfers, offering wetsuit-drying rooms and secure surfboard storage.

Newquay airports, so if the surf's just too good to miss then there's no excuse for the capital's beach bods not to be here.

Watergate Bay

From the A30 or A39, follow the A3059 and then signs to St Mawgan then Newquay.
Coming from Newquay, follow the B3276 coastal road north for just over three miles.

The three miles of exposed, west-facing beach at Watergate Bay are an essential destination for surfers and lovers of all extreme sports. That's not to say this thrills 'n' spills venue isn't for those who simply enjoy walking along, or reclining on, sandy beaches – it's

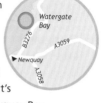

actually a little more laid-back than nearby Newquay Bay. Clifftop walks are easily accessible from Watergate Bay too.

When the tide's out here, the mass of pristine, level sand cries out to be trampled on; it's perfect for users of power kites, kite buggies and any other activity that demands

You haven't really seen Cornwall and its environs until you've taken to the air. A flight from Newquay airport to St Mary's on the Isles of

space. Just ask the people at Extreme Academy, a beach-based company that provides equipment hire and lessons for almost any extreme sport you can think of. If you can't decide which sport to try, maybe the 'Extreme Day' package is for you – your instructor will give you a taster of surfing, kiting, mountain boarding and waveski. There's also a surf shop next door.

When it's all become too much and you need a hot meal or a stiff drink, the Watergate Bay Hotel overlooks the beach. Alternatively, there's The Beach Hut bistro and bar, which offers good-quality food in cosy and relaxed surroundings. For the perfect end to a day on the beach, a plate of local seafood washed down with a refreshing drink is hard to beat, as are Watergate Bay's sea views at sunset.

Scilly is the ultimate bird's eye experience. The trip lasts 25 minutes each way, with time to stop and tour Scilly for a few hours in between.

Porthcothan

The B3276 passes Porthcothan, which is located on the stretch of coastline between Padstow and Newquay.

Porthcothan's beach is perfect for those who simply want to laze under fine skies. Sandwiched between hills and backed by sand dunes, this narrow, sheltered stretch can be a real suntrap. The relatively small, west-facing beach is also used by surfers, but

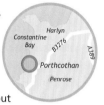

not to the extent of other nearby beaches, such as Constantine Bay (*see* opposite page). Between the car park to the beach and the shore is Porthcothan Bay Stores, which hires out wetsuits, bodyboards, windbreaks and other beach goods.

The coastal path is well signposted in Porthcothan, and a short walk from here to nearby clifftops provides you with some beautiful views of the rural coastal scenery.

Just south of Porthcothan are the Bedruthan Steps – volcanic rock stacks that rise majestically out of the sea at high tide.

Constantine Bay

From the A38, take the A389 towards Padstow. Then take the B3276, from where Constantine Bay is signposted.

Constantine Bay is a wide belt of sandy beach backed by extensive marram-covered dunes. A favourite with surfers, the bay is sandwiched between Booby's Bay to the north and Treyarnon Bay to the south. Lifeguards patrol Constantine Bay, but note that

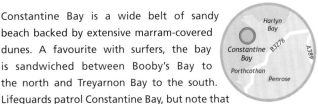

all three of these beaches are considered unsafe for swimming. This beach has a distinctly minimalist feel; its lack of facilities – save for a few shops along the coast road – and sparse features

hint at it having been left exactly as nature intended. The day I visited I saw children running towards the beach armed with fishing nets and then crouching optimistically by the rock pools. Isn't that what beaches should be all about?

Visit nearby Padstow for great shopping or to enjoy lunch at The Seafood Restaurant, owned by celebrity chef Rick Stein.

Harlyn Bay

From the A39 take the A389 towards Padstow. Then join the B3276, from where Harlyn is signposted.

There is no shortage of excellent beaches along this stretch of the Cornish coastline, but Harlyn Bay, close to Padstow, is definitely worth a visit. Sandy and crescent-shaped, the beach is two-thirds of a mile long and enhanced by its serene and natural setting of open fields and valleys.

It's a big hit with families, who generally arrive with plenty of their own supplies, a selection of beach games and an all-important windbreak. However, should you arrive empty-handed, the manned pay booth at the entrance to the car park can sell you everything from a bucket and spade to sunscreen. There is often a mobile café in the car park and, if you're lucky, an ice cream van may pull in to serve you some genuine Cornish fare.

The beach is a popular place to surf and is home to Harlyn Surf School. Lifeguards are on duty during the summer months.

An Iron Age cemetery, which was discovered in the sand behind the beach, has now been turned into a museum.

Polzeath

From the A39 take the B3314 at Wadebridge and continue for approximately
seven miles until you come to Polzeath.

Negotiating the winding country lanes of
Cornwall's north coast is a small price to pay
to reach this fantastic beach by the Camel
Estuary in Hayle Bay. It's a surfers' paradise –
for pros and beginners alike. Lifeguards
patrol the beach during the summer months

and the local Surf Life Saving club is located behind the beach.
Polzeath reveals itself to be a huge area of gently shelving
sandy beach at low tide, when walkers take over from

the surfers; some great
footpaths lead directly
from the beach. You'll find
deckchairs and windbreaks
for hire, and there are
plenty of places to buy the
finest Cornish ice cream.

If you visit Polzeath in the summer keep an eye out
for bottlenose dolphins playing in the coastal waters.

Bude, Summerleaze Beach

From Exeter, follow the A30 dual carriageway. Take the A386 signposted 'Bude', then the A3079 via Halwill. Then take the A3072 via Holsworthy to Bude.

🏠 ⌒ 🍴 🅿 🍷 📷 🛍 🚻

The town of Bude has numerous wonderful sandy beaches that have long been popular with tourists and families. Bude is also a mecca for surfers, who are drawn to the west-facing beaches and their promise of excellent waves. The main Bude beaches are Crooklets, Widemouth Sands, Sandymouth and Summerleaze.

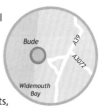

Summerleaze beach

Summerleaze beach is easily accessible as it is the closest beach to the town centre and there's plenty of parking nearby. One of my top 100 beaches, it lies between the town's canal and an area of dunes. It offers an impressive stretch of sand at low tide and there is a large, free swimming pool in the rocks that is filled by the sea at high tide

Take your bikes along to Bude and join the rolling countryside of the Cornish Way – even if you get only as far as the next beach! Those

Bude Haven

and provides safe bathing. Summerleaze gets very busy in the summer – both on the sand and in the sea.

Widemouth Sands, an undulating three-mile walk south of Bude along the clifftops, is zoned to keep bathers and surfers apart. Mainly sandy, at low tide rock pools brimming with life appear, where you might discover a starfish or even a sea slug! Like Summerleaze, lifeguards patrol Widemouth during the summer months. In fact Bude was the first English coastal region to have a Surf Life Saving Club, established in 1953.

The coastal areas surrounding Bude feature fine walking and cycle routes with fantastic sea views and an abundance of wildlife. For sightseeing of another kind, try Bude's busy town centre, with its good choice of pubs, eateries and shops.

looking to step up a gear can always take on the 170-mile route that wriggles its way down the coast from Bude to Land's End.

North East England

Bridlington, North Beach

Well signposted from the A614 and A165. South and North beaches are signposted from the town centre.

The two beaches at Bridlington both offer wide expanses of space at low tide. The sandy South beach may have the aesthetic edge on the pebbly North beach, but the latter has more facilities, is a Blue Flag holder and, for these reasons, is one of my top 100 beaches.

Bridlington was originally a favourite of Yorkshire's wealthy, but the arrival of the railway in the 1840s opened the town up to the masses who quickly acquired a taste for day trips and holidays. I wonder what our

Victorian cousins would make of the jet-skiers and power kiters who grace the shores of South beach today? If a gentle stroll is more your cup of tea, both beaches boast fine stretches of promenade.

If the weather lets you down, the pools at Bridlington Leisure World offer water slides and a wave machine.

Danes Dyke

Leave the A165 near Bridlington and join the B1255. Head towards Flamborough.
Danes Dyke is signposted.

The beach at Danes Dyke is a small, alluring swathe located between Bridlington and Flamborough Head. The area was designated as an English Nature Local Nature Reserve in 2002. You reach the shore by taking a pleasant five-minute stroll along a woodland trail that runs beside a stream.

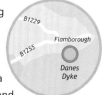

A mixture of sand and pebbles, the beach is backed by cliffs, giving it a well-hidden feel. There is enough sand at low tide to stretch out and relax or enjoy some beach games.

Danes Dyke is great dog-walking country, and canine companions are allowed access to the beach throughout the year. The car park café sells snacks and ice creams, and a picnic area completes the scene.

The fabulous nearby Flamborough Head contains a treasure chest of coves, caves and rock pools to explore.

Filey

Well signposted from the A165 coastal road. Located between Scarborough and Bridlington.

Filey is one of Yorkshire's most popular seaside locations. The bay here is sheltered to the north by a ridge of rocks called Filey Brigg and to the south by the chalk cliffs of Speeton and Bempton. It offers around five miles of pure sandy beach and bathing waters,

which are protected from strong waves by an offshore reef that is accessible at low tide.

Although a smaller resort than neighbouring Scarborough and Bridlington, Filey still has a wide range of facilities to offer. Those shy of the sand can take a walk along the lengthy promenade. At the southern end of the area

The majestic moorland, delightful dales and incredible coastline of the North York Moors National Park are just a

known as Royal Parade are a boating lake and paddling pool, while at the northern end of the promenade you'll find Filey Lifeboat Station, as well as shopping and parking facilities.

The large beach, with its gently sloping smooth, hard sand, ensures that there is generally plenty of space for every visitor, from kite flyers and cricketers to sandcastle builders and deck-chair enthusiasts. However, at high tide on hot summer days, the shore can become a little cramped.

For the more active Fileyphile, the beach is a haven for water-sports fans – take your pick from sailing, windsurfing and kite surfing. Walkers are also in luck: in addition to the National Trails of the Cleveland Way and Wolds Way, there is the shorter Filey Brigg nature trail, as well as Centenary Way.

few miles from Filey. With over 1,400 miles of paths and tracks to explore, North Yorkshire is the perfect place to get out and about.

Scarborough, North Bay

Scarborough is well signposted when approaching from the north and south on the A165 and from the west on the A170 or A64.

Scarborough lays claim to being the first British seaside resort. From as early as the 1620s, visitors arrived here to enjoy the health benefits of its spring water. A century later, the consumption of seawater became all the rage and ensured the ongoing success of the town as a seaside resort. It remains as popular as ever today.

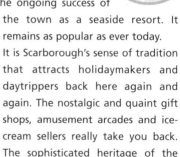

It is Scarborough's sense of tradition that attracts holidaymakers and daytrippers back here again and again. The nostalgic and quaint gift shops, amusement arcades and ice-cream sellers really take you back. The sophisticated heritage of the area is also still very much alive:

South Bay

What has blue blood, three hearts and eight legs? A cephalopod. Scarborough's Sea Life and Marine

where else can you buy freshly cooked lobster on the seafront whilst admiring the beautiful Victorian architecture and grand gardens that Scarborough offers?

The beaches, North Bay

North Bay

and South Bay, are divided by the 12th-century Scarborough Castle, situated at the edge of a cliff and dominating the Scarborough skyline. North Bay, which is a Blue Flag holder and one of my top 100 beaches, is a lifeguard-patrolled zone. A sandy stretch of shore, at high tide the beach isn't as deep as its South Bay sister, but this means a shorter walk to the sea! At low to mid tide, this beach is said to be suitable for those wanting to try their hand at surfing. The beach gets busy in the summer due to its proximity to the town centre, but then don't all the best beaches attract a crowd?

South Bay is a little busier than North Bay. Along with its golden sands and lifeguard patrols, you'll also find the bustling harbour here. During summer months, South Bay has a clearly defined dog-ban zone.

Centre is home to these creatures, as well as sea turtles, octopuses and many more species from the ocean's depths.

Robin Hood's Bay

Located just south of Whitby and well signposted from the A171. Join the B1447 and follow this road to its end.

North Yorkshire's Robin Hood's Bay has the look of a long-forgotten fishing village, with its quaint cottages huddled precariously next to the sea. However, this pretty resort, which dates back to the 1500s, is far from being a quiet backwater and attracts thousands of visitors each year.

Also known as Baytown, the area has always lived off the ocean, but throughout its history this fine fishing tradition has occasionally been interrupted by smugglers. It is said that at one time their contraband of rum, brandy and tobacco could be moved through the village via a maze of tunnels and secret passages without ever seeing the light of day.

The beach at Robin Hood's Bay shouldn't be missed, although it's not recommended that you attempt to drive down to it through the village as the cobbled road is incredibly steep

Movie buffs may recognize nearby Goathland Steam Railway as Hogsmeade Station, one of the stops for J.K. Rowling's Hogwarts

(a 1:3 gradient), with few places to turn around. Instead, there is a large pay and display car park at the top of the hill from where it is a short walk down to the beach. What awaits you is a mixture of flat fissured rocks, boulders and sand, as well as a wealth of rock pools at low tide where you can search out marine life. Defensive walls have been erected to halt the receding shores – a result of incessant waves lashing the coast – and protect the whitewashed cottages and the town behind them. To really appreciate the beach though, I suggest walking up onto the nearby cliffs and taking it all in from there. The view looking north from Ravenscar on a sunny day is immense, so it's no surprise that Robin Hood's Bay is part of the stunning North York Moors National Park.

There are many tales and myths told as to how Robin Hood's Bay got its name, but no one knows for certain. Maybe he just fell in love with the beach.

Express in the Harry Potter films. Just don't go looking for platform 9¾ – that was filmed at London's King's Cross.

Whitby, West Cliff

Well signposted from both the A174 and A171. Arriving via the A169, after driving through the village of Sleights turn right at the roundabout and follow signs to Whitby.

For a small port lying on the northeast coast, Whitby is big on history. One of its most famous residents was the explorer Captain James Cook, who lived here during the early part of his life. He arrived in Whitby in 1746 as an apprentice to a shipowner and, consequently,

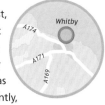

a number of vessels built here were used for Cook's voyages. Whitby is also well known for its association with the story of Dracula. Not only did Bram Stoker allegedly write the tale

while staying in Whitby, but also various parts of the town are featured in the book.

Losing yourself in Whitby's history is one thing, but you're just as likely to find yourself lost among its winding streets. Once you've

Whitby's Magpie Cafe, with its distinctive black-and-white facade, serves some of the best seafood in

got your bearings back, however, a short walk from the harbour will lead you to West Cliff – more than two miles of sandy and rocky beach sheltered by steep cliffs. Kept free of litter throughout the year, the sea is typically safe for bathing. The beach has parking, toilets

and a first-aid point and is patrolled by a lifeguard during the summer months. Whitby also possesses twin piers – West pier and East pier – which lie only a matter of metres from each other and are both adorned with (non-working) lighthouses. Pay a small fee and you can climb the West pier lighthouse.

For those who don't want to walk, it is possible to reach the beach from the top of the cliff using the Cliff Lift, which delivers you straight to the shore – most unusual! For those who *do* fancy a walk, there are always the 199 steps to climb from the town to St Mary's church and the abbey. It's worth the trek, and by the time you're done all that sea air will have given you an appetite for some famous Whitby fish and chips!

North Yorkshire. If you're hungry then make sure you arrive early as the long queues are almost as famous as the fare!

Kettleness Sands

Follow signs for Runswick Bay from the A174 coastal road. To reach the beach follow the Cleveland Way footpath in the direction of Whitby.

Kettleness is predominantly a beach for fossil hunters wanting to explore the best of Yorkshire's Jurassic Coast. Those in search of a sandy beach should head a little further north to the shores of Runswick Bay.

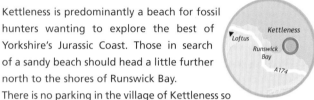

There is no parking in the village of Kettleness so you're best off driving to Runswick Bay and walking back the 1.5 miles along the Cleveland Way clifftop path, which is a treat in itself. Be careful of the sheer drops along the way though, especially when admiring the fantastic views. And once you reach the beach, note that the tide sweeps in very quickly here. Among the beautiful surroundings here you'll notice areas of what look like brown lunar landscape. These are alum shale excavations. From the early 17th century onwards, alum was a vital ingredient in two industries in this region – textiles and tanning. What you see are the by-products of this era.

The Cleveland Way is a 110-mile horseshoe-shaped route around the edge of the North York Moors National Park.

Runswick Bay

Runswick is clearly signposted from the A174. Once in Runswick, follow the signs for the bay and the car park.

The sand and shingle arc of Runswick Bay is situated eight miles northwest of Whitby. Follow the signs to the beach down a very steep road and there you'll find the sheltered bay, overlooked by the village's tiny cottages. Suitable for families, the beach also attracts water-sports enthusiasts, hence the elevated blue building

that is the Runswick Bay Beach & Sailing Club. Swimming is generally safe, and when conditions are right you can surf here. Budding marine biologists among you will enjoy the rock pools that appear at low tide at either end of the bay, and walkers can pick up the Cleveland Way from here.

North of Runswick Bay is Boulby Cliff – the highest cliff on the east coast of England, standing at 200m (660ft).

Staithes

Signposted from the A174 coastal road, but keep your eyes peeled as the entrance to the village is easily missed.

Tucked into a cleft of rock that forms a natural harbour in this rugged patch of coastline, Staithes is a genuine working fishing village. The beach is compact, sheltered and consists mainly of sand with a smattering of rock pools. To try to halt coastal erosion, the cliff face here has been shored up with 50,000 tons of Norwegian rock.

From the pay and display car park at the entrance to the village, it is a five-minute walk along the narrow cobbled street

down to the beach – don't try to drive right down to the shore as there's little room for cars!

Head across to the harbour and take a look at the cobles, the traditional fishing vessels used to catch local cod, lobster and crab.

Those of a nautical disposition might like to check out the Captain Cook and Staithes Heritage Centre on the high street.

Marsden Bay

Located on the A183 coastal road. The car park is clearly signposted from the road.

Marsden Bay offers a surprisingly dramatic setting for a beach in what is essentially an urban location between South Shields and Sunderland. The bay is best known for the 42m (139ft) high Marsden Rock, home to kittiwakes, cormorants and fulmars. The beach

is a brilliant arc of sand and shingle, sheltered by cliffs and accessed down steep steps.

Built into caves in the cliffs is a spectacular-looking restaurant, Tavistock at the Grotto, which you access via a lift. If a picnic is

more your scene, then the clifftop is the ideal setting, with views south of the red-and-white striped Souter Lighthouse at Lizard Point, owned by the National Trust.

Want to get back to nature? Marsden Old Quarry Local Nature Reserve is situated just opposite Lizard Lane caravan park.

Druridge Bay

Follow signs for Druridge Country Park from the A1068 – the beach and visitor centre are well signposted.

Druridge Bay is a beautiful rural beach, backed for part of its length by Druridge Bay Country Park. In 1995 the area was designated as part of the North Northumberland Heritage Coast, and the beach and dunes are a Site of Special Scientific Interest.

The coastal scenery here is astounding: golden sands, brimming pools and lush reedbeds are the perfect habitat for a wealth of bird life (as well as picnicking humans). The country park also includes a lake – Lake Ladyburn – which can be used for

sailing, windsurfing and canoeing. If you fancy an ice cream, the visitor centre, just a few hundred metres from the beach, has a small shop and café open daily 11–4 during the school holidays.

In the summer, Druridge Bay Country Park holds sailing, canoeing and windsurfing courses for children (8–16 years).

98

Low Hauxley

From the A1 at Alnwick join the A1068. Follow the road south until you see signs for Hauxley and Amble. Then come off at the coastal road.

A gem of a beach, Low Hauxley is as popular with local residents as it is with out-of-towners. Sitting pretty between Amble and Druridge Bay, this spotless sandy beach is typically a peaceful place to enjoy a walk by the sea, relax in the sun or compete in a couple

of favourite beach games. It is also a popular place with kite landboarders, who take advantage of the flat, compact stretches of sand presented when the tide's out.

A short distance offshore you'll spy Coquet Island and its

lighthouse, owned by the Duke of Northumberland and managed by the RSPB as a nature reserve. More than 30,000 pairs of seabirds nest here each year, including puffins and terns.

Boat trips to Coquet Island operate from Amble throughout the summer, but to protect the bird life you cannot land there.

Warkworth

The main access to the beach is signposted from the town centre – in the direction of the golf course.

Lying in the loop of the River Coquet on the Heritage Coast, Warkworth is a pretty village dominated by the dramatic ruins of its 12th-century castle. It is further blessed with a beautiful stretch of beach that extends the length of Alnmouth Bay, offering long, golden sweeping sands. Backed by dunes and shelving steadily to the sea, the beach also comprises a vast extent of compacted sand, which is perfect for beach games and walking. After the ebb tide, rock pools at the northern end of the beach contain all sorts of fascinating sea creatures. The main access to the beach is signposted from the centre of the town. From the free car park it is a good ten-minute walk along a sandy path, which snakes through the dunes. Although it manages to retain a rural, natural feel, the beach is very popular and does get busy in summer.

In need of a little sanctuary? Then fear not because close to the castle is Warkworth Hermitage – a small cave cut from the rocky side

Those in the know, who are keen to avoid the trek and find a more peaceful stretch of beach, use the public footpath that cuts though the golf course. This is accessed from the end of a short road situated on the right-hand side of the A1086, about half a mile to the north of the town. It is not clearly signposted so keep your eyes peeled!

Away from the beach, the village of Warkworth offers a good selection of pubs, cafés and gift shops within its charming little streets, so take some time to wander and peruse. A visit to English Heritage-owned Warkworth Castle is a must: this hillside stronghold was home to the powerful Percy family of Shakespearean fame, and the film *Elizabeth,* starring Cate Blanchett and Joseph Fiennes, was set here.

of the River Coquet. This secluded hideaway can be reached only by being rowed across the river by boat.

Alnmouth

Follow signs for Alnmouth from the A1 or the A1068 coastal road. Then follow signs for the old village and car parks.

For several centuries the coastal village of Alnmouth was a prosperous port, shipping out stone, grain, wool, sheepskin and leather while importing tea, coffee, oranges and lemons. The last ship sailed from Alnmouth in 1896, but fishing continues in the area.

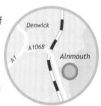

Rail passengers on the East Coast main line enjoy fleeting views of this beautiful spot as they travel between Newcastle and Edinburgh. Perched on a tongue of land formed by the sea and the River Aln, this lovely seaside destination remains

uncommercialized but does get busy in summer. The mainly sandy beach is a short walk from the village where there are nearby areas of grass suitable for picnics.

Nearby Alnwick Castle is the second largest inhabited castle in England. The largest? That'll be Windsor Castle.

Boulmer Haven

From Alnwick, follow the A1068 to Lesbury and then signs to Boulmer
along the coast road.

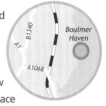

The small coastal village of Boulmer is situated
between Lesbury and Longhoughton. Its
beautiful and unspoilt beach is made up of
predominantly soft white sand. The shore is
also dotted with large pebbles, and at low
tide a rocky reef is revealed, proving a great place
to search for sponges, sea firs and soft coral. Anchored cobles –
local fishing boats – can often be seen swaying in the bay's

waters, as there is no harbour here.
The beach also has no shops or
cafés, so take your own supplies if
you intend to eat there; you'll find
areas of grass behind the beach
suitable for picnics. Alternatively,
you can always head for Boulmer
village's Fishing Boat Inn.

**Just north of Boulmer is 18th-century Howick Hall – a
gardener's paradise full of rare and fascinating plants.**

Embleton Bay

Follow signs for Embleton from the B1339. Drive through the village towards Dunstanburgh Castle Golf Course.

This is a classic rural Northumberland beach with a wide expanse of powdery golden sand backed by dunes. The views along the curve of the bay are made all the more beautiful by the silhouette of the ruins of Dunstanburgh Castle at the southern end.

You access the mile-long beach by taking a short walk across Dunstanburgh Castle Golf Course. There are no facilities at the beach although the golf course does have a bar and restaurant

that are open to the public.

Sea conditions at this National Trust-owned bay are often unsuitable for swimming, but its sheer beauty, panoramic views, wondrous walks and lustrous sands can't fail to keep allcomers happily occupied.

Visit the nearby attractive port of Craster, where it is still possible to buy freshly smoked kippers from the harbourside.

Low Newton-by-the-Sea

Follow signs from the B1339 coastal road for the village of Low Newton. Drive through the village and follow signs down to Low Newton-by-the-Sea.

Low Newton-by-the-Sea is an idyllic sheltered beach lying between Bamburgh and Alnmouth. The area of Newton-by-the-Sea is almost entirely owned by the National Trust. Remote and rural, the location of the beach may give you the impression that

you've discovered it for yourself, but don't be fooled as in the summer it can get very busy and parking can be difficult. The small, sandy beach is protected by an offshore reef, making

it an ideal bathing spot. As you'd expect, swimming conditions are calm. When you're all beached out, pop into the picturesque 18th-century village and have a drink and a bite to eat at the bustling Ship Inn. Alternatively, enjoy a picnic on the village green in Newton Square.

A short drive north brings you to the town of Seahouses – go there for the ultimate fish-and-chip experience.

Beadnell Bay

Follow signs for Beadnell from the B1340 coastal road or the A1. The beach and car park are well signposted.

Beadnell Bay is a wonderful sandy beach situated on the Northumberland Heritage Coastline between Bamburgh and Embleton. Fringed with dunes, its sheer size – over two miles in length – means it's never likely to become overcrowded on hot summer days.

A big hit with families, who love the seemingly endless clean sands, the bay's reliable winds and easy beach access also attract windsurfers and sailing enthusiasts. Swimming

conditions are pleasant, the coast's shipwrecks are a magnet to divers, and canoeists and sea kayaks can often be seen zipping through the waters.

Beadnell's harbour is the only one on the east coast to face west, so stick around for some spectacular sunsets.

Ornithologists will delight in Beadnell's natural dune habitats and bird sanctuaries. Look out for eider, scoter and wigeon.

Bamburgh

Clearly signposted from the A1 and B1341. Just after you pass Bamburgh Castle take the Wyndings turn-off to the car park.

Despite its beauty, the beach at Bamburgh is one of few where you will find yourself more inclined to look inland than out to sea. This is, of course, as a result of the imposing Bamburgh Castle, which sits on an elevated, rocky outcrop directly behind the beach. Visit it for fine views of Holy Island and the Farne Islands.

The beach can be accessed from various parts of the village and offers a large expanse of beautiful golden sand backed by

dunes. The bay is very clean and generally uncrowded, and at low tide you'll find exposed rock pools, ready for exploration.

A unique way to survey the beach is by horse, and bookings can be made locally.

Bamburgh is home to the famous Copper Kettle tea rooms – after a day on the beach, pop in for an afternoon pick-me-up.

Holy Island

Clearly signposted from the A1. Heading north, turn right onto the unclassified road through Beal. You reach the island via a causeway.

Often referred to by its ancient name of Lindisfarne, Holy Island is best known for its links to Christianity and the Lindisfarne priory and castle. In 635AD, the Irish evangelist St Aidan founded a monastic community that became one of the most important centres of Christianity in Anglo-Saxon England. Viking raids finally forced the monks to abandon the island in 875, but in 1082 the Benedictines rebuilt the priory, the remains of

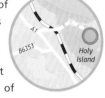

which can be visited today.

Holy Island is located just south of Berwick-upon-Tweed and is only accessible at low tide, when a man-made causeway is revealed from beneath the water, making it possible to walk

Lost track of time during your visit to Holy Island and now waiting for the tide to turn? A visit to St Aidan's Winery will while away an

or drive across from the mainland. Even before the causeway was built in 1954, this was regarded as one of the safest routes to the island and is said

to have been used as a crossing point for over 1,000 years.

At low tide, if you walk across the huge dunes that run alongside the main access road, you'll discover what seems to be an infinite expanse of pristine sand extending north from the island – truly a remarkable sight. Parts of the beach are sheltered by the dunes, but otherwise the area is very exposed. There is also a small pebbly beach near the centre of the village. Beyond the beaches, Holy Island has a number of other attractions well worth visiting. Managed by English Heritage, the ancient priory houses an award-winning museum. Lindisfarne Castle, which is a National Trust property, is also open to the public throughout the summer. Be aware, though, that opening times can vary due to the tides, which render the causeway impassable for two hours before high tide and three hours after, thus temporarily restoring the area's island status.

hour or two. Here you can sample the world-famous Lindisfarne Mead, made from fermented white grapes, honey, herbs and water.

North West England

Southport

Located on the A565 between Liverpool and Preston. Coming from the southwest, take the A570 from Ormskirk.

Victorian Southport has a long tradition of entertaining the residents of the North West, but those from further afield should think about paying this part of the Sefton Coast a visit too. Matching this long tradition is the impressive seafront – the coastline extends for 22 miles from Southport in the north to Crosby in the south.

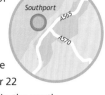

Southport beach has all you require for a perfect day out: plenty of room for car owners to park up and enjoy the panoramic views, golden sands, designated bathing areas (with a first-aid point and lifeguards on patrol during the summer), amusement arcades, crazy golf and much

Finding the beach a little too sedate? Then check out more than 60 rides and attractions at Southport's Pleasureland

more. Those looking for high-speed thrills should head further south to Ainsdale beach and try their hand at kite buggying (pictured right).

The seafront has undergone extensive restoration in the last few years. Wander along the promenade, stopping to appreciate the majestic beauty of King's Gardens and the bronze statue of Queen Victoria. A new sea wall, Marine Drive, has been built to halt the flooding that used to plague Southport. And a cool £7 million has been invested in Southport's pier, which at 1,100m (3,600ft) is the second longest in Britain after Southend-on-Sea.

Catch the Southport Roadtrain to get around, or maybe the horse-drawn Landau carriages are more to your liking.

amusement park. For those brave enough, The Traumatizer is the UK's tallest, fastest suspended looping rollercoaster.

Blackpool

Leave the M6 at Junction 32 and join the M55. Come off the M55 at Junction 4 and join the A583. You will then meet the A584 coastal road.

The sheer scale of the seaside resort of Blackpool is evident long before you reach the coast. Not only does it adjoin the M6 via its own motorway – the M55 – but its iconic tower and giant rollercoaster are visible from absolutely miles away.

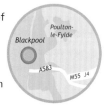

Blackpool offers the traditional and stereotypical seaside holiday experience in excess, and nowhere else, apart from Blackpool Pleasure Beach, can boast being Britain's most visited

It was in 1885 that Blackpool's first electric tram rolled into action along Princess Street. You can still capture the charm

free tourist attraction, welcoming over 11 million visitors annually.

The seven miles of sandy beach that make up the North and South shores have come a long way since Blackpool was just a mere 18th-century village. Today, the famous  Golden Mile covers the strip of road in the central beach area between the North and Central piers, renowned for its illuminations, amusement arcades, tram and donkey rides, kiss-me-quick hats, pubs, fish and chip shops and bingo halls. The beach is cleaned daily, the quality of bathing water has improved in recent years and beach patrols operate throughout the year. On a busy summer's day more than 5,000 deck chairs and sun loungers are hired out for use on the beach.

After strolling down one of three piers, take the weight off your feet by catching the lift to the top of the celebrated Blackpool Tower. From here, you can enjoy a bird's-eye view of Blackpool Pleasure Beach, home to the tallest and fastest rollercoaster in Europe, the Pepsi Big One. Over 60m (200ft) high, this ride hurtles thrill seekers along more than a mile of track at speeds of up to 87mph. Not for the faint-hearted.

and sense of nostalgia today by hopping aboard any one of the 65 cars that travel along the 12 miles of line.

Haverigg

Follow signs for Haverigg from the main A595 and then the A5093. Drive through the village to reach the beach and car park.

Close to the town of Millom on the fringe of Cumbria's Lake District National Park, Haverigg is a pretty, rural beach. If it isn't attracting walkers across its sands, then it's keeping water-sports enthusiasts busy. At high tide the beach is reasonably limited in

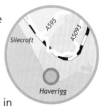

size, but at low tide the sea pushes out to leave ample space between the sand dunes and lapping waves. Behind the dunes is a children's playground, a picnic area, a handy beach shop and a café.

To the east of the beach is the sea wall of Hodbarrow Lagoon, originally part of an iron ore mine, and now an important bird reserve.

Head inland along the A593 and you'll soon arrive at beautiful Coniston Water. The walks around the lake are magnificent.

Silecroft

The beach is just off the A595 and lies three miles northeast of Millom. Follow signs for Silecroft and Whicham.

A few miles north of Haverigg and lying just within the Lake District National Park, Silecroft offers the visitor several miles of mainly shingle beach backed by fields. This perfect coming together of coast and countryside is encapsulated in the half-mile drive that takes you from the small village of Silecroft to the shore. The beach is kept tidy and is zoned: windsurfers and waterskiers are restricted to the northern end; the southern part of the beach is a designated bathing area, where gently shelving sands provide ideal conditions for swimming. Groups of canoeists often congregate at Silecroft, and there is also a launching bay for deep-water fishing.

Silecroft Caravan & Camping Park is a minute's walk from the beach and you'll spot many a happy camper beachcombing, walking the coast or enjoying one of the area's beautiful sunsets.

The ascent up Black Combe mountain begins a mile from Silecroft. Peaking at 2,000m (600ft), the views are sensational.

Ravenglass

Ravenglass is signposted from the A595. The beach is accessible from numerous points along the main street.

In Roman times the attractive hamlet of Ravenglass was a bustling port. Today, it is better known as the starting point of the seven-mile line of the Ravenglass and Eskdale narrow-gauge steam railway.

The meeting of the rivers Irt, Mite and Esk in Ravenglass forms an estuary which fills at high tide and covers the beach and areas of mud flats. This a beautiful place for a peaceful stroll – the dunes around Ravenglass and the

beach are nature reserves, with the area being rich in animal and plant life. Inland there are also exquisite woodland walks. The best areas of sandy beach are difficult to locate, so you might want to ask a local for help. Swimming isn't recommended here.

A short drive away is the allegedly haunted Muncaster Castle, home of the Pennington family for over 800 years.

St Bees

Follow signs for St Bees from the main A595. The beach is to the west of the village and lies three miles from Whitehaven and Egremont.

Surrounded by fields, you reach this popular family beach by driving through the idyllic ancient village of St Bees, famous for its public school and priory church.

As is typical along this stretch of coast, extensive areas of sand almost disappear at high tide, leaving just a band of shingle. At low tide, however, rock pools can be found at the foot of St Bees Head. St Bees is also the start (or end, depending on your preference) of the scenic Coast to Coast Walk, a challenging 190-mile route

linking St Bees to Robin Hood's Bay on the Yorkshire coast. Taking 12 to 14 days, this mammoth adventure passes through three National Parks – the Lake District, Yorkshire Dales and North York Moors.

Facial contortionists, listen up! Every September the nearby Egremont Crab Fair hosts the World Gurning Championships.

Allonby

Allonby is situated four miles north of Maryport on the B5300 coastal road leading to Silloth.

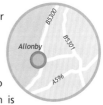

Allonby is one of Cumbria's most popular beaches – and with good reason. It is a long and picturesque rural beach that offers exceptional views both across the Solway Firth estuary towards Scotland and inland to the hills of the Lake District. Allonby beach is also a great place to enjoy stunning sunsets all year round, but is at its most spectacular on warm summer's evenings.

Allonby is part of the Solway Coast Area of Outstanding Natural Beauty, and the village of Allonby has conservation area status. The local ice cream shop, which faces the beach, is also a major attraction as it sells a number of delicious home-made varieties, as well as a few other beach essentials.

Sand and shingle are the order of the day on Allonby beach. A regular haunt for bathers, the northern end of the shore is also known as an excellent sea-fishing location.

Sticking with the marine theme, the Lake District Coast Aquarium at nearby Maryport invites you to stroke friendly

For the sporty, reliable wind conditions keep windsurfers and kite surfers coming back throughout the year. However, conditions are said to be best suited to the more experienced, and water sport activities should be restricted to periods of high tide only.

At the busiest times of the year, when the beach is a brimming with walkers and bathers, those in the know who prefer a more peaceful place to relax won't stop at one of Allonby's numerous free car parks; instead they'll continue north along the coast road for a couple of miles to the village of Mawbray where access to a quieter stretch of shore can be found.

Near to Allonby is the attractive market town of Cockermouth, where the River Cocker meets the River Derwent. In addition to being the birthplace of William Wordsworth, Cockermouth offers plenty in the way of shops, restaurants, supermarkets and accommodation.

rays, gaze down at glass walkways containing sharks, gurnard and turbot, and touch starfish and sea anemones in rock pools.

Silloth, Silloth West

From Maryport, head north. Silloth beach and Silloth West beach are well signposted on arrival at the town on the B5300.

Located in northern Cumbria and with a history dating back to the 1850s, the imaginative planning that went into the town of Silloth clearly shows in its wide, elegant streets, spacious seafront green and splendid promenade stretching north towards Skinburness. It has enviable beaches too, boasting clean sands and pure waters, a wildlife habitat and facilities including a children's playground and picnic area.

Lying between the town centre and the promenade, Silloth's green is a hive of activity all year round. There's the vintage

Nestling on the shores of the Solway Firth and facing the hills of Dumfries & Galloway, Silloth West is one of my top 100 beaches. Spacious, sandy, gently shelving and backed by dunes, it is protected from the elements by a man-made sea defence of massive rocks. It's a favourite of windsurfers, canoeists, anglers and cyclists.

Nearby Silloth beach is a large sand-and-shingle stretch. Regrettably, the image of this gorgeous coast is tarnished a little at high tide when the beach almost disappears, and there are signs warning that the waters are not safe for bathing. Still, at least the green behind the beach provides a paddling pool, sand pit, crazy golf and other activities to keep you busy. Silloth Carnival is also held here annually in August.

rally in June, a kite festival is held every July, and the Silloth Beer Festival delivers an annual brew or two in September.

Wales

Porthcawl, Rest Bay

Follow signs to Porthcawl from Junction 37 of the M4. Rest Bay is well signposted as you approach the town.

Porthcawl boasts award-winning, clean, sandy beaches at Sandy Bay, Trecco Bay and the quieter Rest Bay. Just a stone's throw from the M4, Rest Bay entices you in to relax on grassy Lock's Common or to explore the secluded sands. A good tip to avoid the queue

for the beach car park is to take the 'Porthcawl Princess' – the road train that runs from Coney Beach to Rest Bay and back. During summer local families and holidaymakers make the most of the pristine beach and surroundings. The long stretch of coast here offers plenty of space at low tide and is backed by rocks providing shelter and broad areas of grass – ideal for picnics. There is also a lifeguard station situated behind the beach.

It's a common sight to see surfers dashing barefoot from the car park to the beach as west-facing Rest Bay has a reputation for being one of the best surf beaches in the area.

Not far from Porthcawl are the Kenfig Dunes, a nature reserve of wetlands, scrub and sand dunes.

Oxwich Bay

Leave the M4 at Junction 42 and follow the A483 to Swansea. Then join the A4118 South Gower Road. Oxwich Bay is clearly signposted.

One of many appealing sandy beaches on the stunningly beautiful Gower Peninsula, Oxwich Bay is more popular than surrounding beaches because of its great accessibility and good facilities. Although relatively sheltered and considered safe for bathing, there are no lifeguards on duty and the beach has a slipway that is used by water-sports enthusiasts, so all visitors should take extra care. Oxwich is well known for its National Nature Reserve, which contains a wide range of protected habitats including

foreshore, dunes, marsh and woodland – in fact the whole of the peninsula has been declared an Area of Outstanding Natural Beauty since 1956.

The Gower Heritage Centre on the South Gower Road is a rural-life museum based around a working 12th-century water mill.

Rhossili Bay

From Swansea, take the A4118 South Gower Road before joining the B4247.
Rhossili Bay is clearly signposted.

This is undoubtedly one of Britain's most magnificent beaches – Rhossili Bay really has to be seen to be believed. Situated on the far western tip of the Gower Peninsula, it's the landscape you'll have seen in just about every tourist advert for Wales. From the point at

which most visitors arrive, the first glimpse of the beach is of the dramatic view from the clifftop down to the shore, seemingly stretching away forever.

Rhossili Bay offers miles of clean sand with enough space to

accommodate everybody, from kite flyers to sunbathers and walkers. The beach even has its own shipwreck – the remains of the Helvetia, wrecked in 1887. As the beach has consistently good waves, it also attracts surfers in droves, which is why

The southern tip of the bay points out towards Worm's Head, a steep, green island with a rearing seaward head that is truly

the Welsh Surfing Federation Surf School operates from nearby Llangennith during the summer months. Facilities at Rhossili are good and you'll find numerous places to eat and drink. Particularly appealing is the terrace at the Worm's Head Hotel, where you can take

in the spectacular views along the full length of the coastline while enjoying a refreshing drink or two.

The National Trust owns and manages much of the land on the Gower Peninsula. You'll find the trust's Rhossili visitor centre, which was once the old Coastguard Cottage, close to the beach. Pop in and learn a little more about the area.

Be aware that there is a long series of steps down to the beach, which may prove problematic for young children on the climb back up at the end of the day.

evocative of its Viking name *wurm*, or dragon. Take care if you visit though – it's a notoriously dangerous causeway.

Cefn Sidan

Off Junction 48 of the M4. Located west of Llanelli on the A484 Llanelli to Carmarthen coast road.

Cefn Sidan (*silk back*) is a seemingly infinite expanse of soft golden sand in a pristine, natural setting. A European Blue Flag winner, the beach offers superb views of the Gower Peninsula, Britain's first designated Area of Outstanding Natural Beauty. Sections safe for swimming are zoned, and lifeguards are on duty during the summer months.

The eight miles of beach are backed by deep dunes, behind

which is Pembrey Country Park, providing 200ha (500 acres) of pine forest, wildlife trails and picnic areas. Dogs are banned from the main beach during the summer. Walkers, however, are welcome year-round to roam the often-deserted expanse that Cefn Sidan has to offer.

TV car nut Jeremy Clarkson: "If Cefn Sidan was for sale I'd buy it. It's eight miles long – perfect for car testing."

Saundersfoot

From the M4, drive on until the road changes to the A48. The A48 turns into the A40 at Carmarthen. Continue and join the A477. Saundersfoot is signposted from here.

Part of the Pembrokeshire Coast National Park and located three miles from Tenby, Saundersfoot is a small, attractive fishing village with a busy beach and harbour. Despite relative modernization, it has managed to successfully retain its charm while providing all the essential ingredients for a family seaside holiday, including water sports and fishing, gift shops and B&Bs,

and a seafood restaurant overlooking the coast.

The beach shelves gently into the sea, making it ideal for a paddle, while the fine, golden sand will keep the most enthusiastic sandcastle-maker content.

Nearby Pendine Sands is where Sir Malcolm Campbell achieved three land speed records in the 1920s.

Barafundle Bay

From the unclassified road linking Freshwater East and Stackpole, follow the brown heritage signs for Stackpole Quay.

Situated in the Pembrokeshire Coast National Park, Barafundle Bay is an idyllic rural beach. Characterized by limestone cliffs, the clean, sandy shoreline is tucked away in a serene location and offers safe bathing conditions. This part of the coastline is also popular for water sports, including canoeing, windsurfing and scuba diving. Barafundle Bay is sufficiently off the beaten track to ensure that it remains unspoilt: there isn't a whiff of an ice cream

van, donkey ride, chippy or beachside shop, meaning it's definitely one for the purist. However, as the beach lies within the National Trust-owned Stackpole Estate, there are decent nearby facilities, such as a toilet block, car park and café.

Stackpole Estate is a sprawling 325ha (800 acre) blanket of green and pleasant land. The estate's lakes are a big draw too,

To reach the beach, park in the Stackpole Quay car park. From here it is just a 10-minute walk along a clifftop path to the shore, enjoying magnificent sea views (usually a turquoise blue) as you go. Think of this stroll as an appetizer to take the edge off your hunger before you feast on the main course to come. There's a small price to pay for this kind of secluded beauty though, and that's the steep descent down to the coast – the only access point – so take great care as you go.

There are no facilities on the actual beach so take your own supplies. If it's walking you hanker for, then you'll appreciate the Pembrokeshire Coast Path lying parallel to the beach – from here you can enjoy stunning, well-signposted routes in either direction.

Dogs are allowed on the beach, and waste bags are supplied at the car park.

with otters, herons, waterfowl and dragonflies – including the rare Hairy Dragonfly – being the star attractions.

Whitesand Bay

The A487 roads from the north and south meet at St David's. Whitesand Bay is clearly signposted from here. Simply follow the B4583.

Most of Pembrokeshire's coastline consists of rugged cliffs and coves broken up by some of the best sandy beaches in Wales. Whitesand Bay is one of the very best. Lying just north of the city of St David's, it is set in a fantastic area of pristine, natural beauty.

The waves at this west-facing sandy beach are consistently impressive, which is why you'll often see plenty of surfers bobbing in the water or riding the waves – surf lessons were taking place on the day I visited. There are also clearly

marked zones for bathing and other water sports.

The atmosphere here is relaxed and friendly, a feeling generated mainly by the excited surf dudes preparing to hit the water, or

Try and allow time to continue northwards along the coast to the beautiful cove of Mwnt. Bottlenose dolphins sometimes

those relaxing, post-surf, outside the combined café and shop by the shore. Recently revamped, this place sells some of the best ice cream around and is an essential pitstop on hot summer days. Adorning the walls of the café are some fascinating storyboards describing how the region has evolved and what kinds of plant and animal wildlife can be spotted locally.

Opposite the car park you can pick up the coastal path, which makes for an interesting circular walk and provides great views over the bay. On hairier parts of the path you'll need to hold onto young children and keep dogs on leads.

Whitesand Bay's popularity can cause problems during the summer when the access road, car park and surf become crowded, so just stay patient, smile and enjoy the hot weather!

feed and play in the waters here, and it is estimated that in the summer Cardigan Bay contains up to 400 of them.

Harlech

This stretch of coast can be accessed at various points along the A496 between Harlech and Llanbedrog.

Lying beneath the towering stone walls of 13th-century Harlech Castle, this is a popular and picturesque sandy beach backed by a collection of dunes. Rich in wildlife and maritime history, the shoreline falls within Snowdonia National Park.

At the southern end of Harlech beach is Shell Island, actually a small peninsula and aptly named because it is said that there are more than 200 types of shell to be found there. The peninsula has three beaches, and you should time your visit

carefully as there's a danger of being stranded at high tide. Harlech Castle, a World Heritage Site, is one of the great fortresses that Edward I built to enforce his rule over the Welsh.

Harlech's impressive backdrop is the Rhinog mountain range – some of the most rugged and remote terrain in Wales.

Llanbedrog

Located between Pwllheli and Abersoch on the A499, which runs along the south coast of the Lleyn Peninsula.

National Trust-owned Llanbedrog beach is rural, sandy and reached along an inviting lane with a stream running parallel to it. A small restaurant overlooks the shore, which is the perfect place to take a break and watch the coastal world go by.

It must be stressed that the Lleyn Peninsula is blessed with numerous excellent beaches and to visit just one would

be a real pity. Recommended beaches on the south coast include nearby Abersoch and, further west, the top surf spot of Hell's Mouth. You'll find the most westerly beach on the peninsula in the lovely old fishing village of Aberdaron.

Nearby Porth Oer beach is also known as Whistling Sands owing to the eerie noises that can be heard as you walk along it.

Llanddwyn Bay

Follow signs from Newborough's main street, which is on the A4080. The turn-off towards Newborough Forest can be easily missed so keep an eye out.

Llanddwyn Bay is a spectacular sweep of sand on the southern coast of the Isle of Anglesey. Access to the beach is through a Forestry Commission toll road of protected Corsican pines – better known as Newborough Forest – which is home to a wide range of plants and birds. Today it is especially a haven for red squirrels, but before the woodland was planted 60 years ago, this used to be all dunes.

The main car park is located directly behind the beach, but there are numerous other places to park that offer easy access to this stretch of unkempt shoreline. There are well-signposted walking trails of varying lengths in the forest, and a leisurely stroll to nearby Llanddwyn Island –

The Isle of Anglesey is bordered by over 100 miles of coastline – enough to start you off. The island is

with its lighthouse and other historical sites of interest – is highly recommended.

Llanddwyn Bay's soft sand stretches for several miles, and your visit will be rewarded with some fine views of the Lleyn Peninsula and Snowdonia National Park. The sunsets in this neck of the woods can be something a little bit special too.

Facilities at the beach are fairly limited so bring along food and drink. There are toilets at the main car park, and beach wardens are on hand during the summer months to assist with basic first-aid needs.

The bay's beach shelves gently into the sea, and conditions are typically safe for swimming and water sports. Dogs are banned during the summer from the stretch of shore between the main beach entrance and Llanddwyn Island, but they can be exercised on other sections along the coast.

known locally as Môn Mam Cymru – the Mother of Wales – a reference to its historical role as the country's bread basket.

Red Wharf Bay

Once on the Isle of Anglesey, take the A5025 turning from the A55. Red Wharf Bay is signposted and located between Pentraeth and Benllech.

A picture-postcard coastal area on the northern shore of the Isle of Anglesey, this undeveloped bay has a peaceful atmosphere and is surrounded by wooded slopes.

Red Wharf Bay

Llanbedrgoch

Pentraeth

A5025

At low tide a vast, sandy area is exposed, making the sea appear – depending on your mood – either rather distant and inaccessible or a challenging yet rewarding walk away. If you're not feeling energetic, just

behind the beach is the Old Boathouse – a restaurant and café that is the perfect spot to wait for the tide to return. When the weather's bad, pull up a chair by the roaring fire in the Ship Inn pub, located behind the beach. Walkers will love the choice of coastal routes that can be joined from the bay.

Lanfairpwllgwyngyllgogerychwyrndrobwllllantysiliogogogoch village in Anglesey has the longest place name in Britain.

Llandudno, North Shore

Accessible from the east and west along the A55 trunk road, which links Chester and Holyhead.

Llandudno is Wales' largest resort, situated between the Great and Little Ormes with two wonderful beaches: the vibrant North Shore and the quiet, sand-duned West Shore. One of my top 100 beaches, North Shore consists of a long crescent of sand sheltered by

rocky headlands. Here you'll find a well-preserved pier, a large promenade and grand terraces of hotels and shopping streets. The beach at West Shore sits in the estuary of the River

Conwy and is less developed. Dotted with dunes, groynes and mudflats, there is also a long promenade and a children's play area. Wind- and kite surfers are catered for, with zoning in place.

For great views of Llandudno, take the tramway to the top of the Great Orme from Church Walks near the pier.

Scotland

Yellowcraig

Yellowcraig is signposted from the A198 coastal road. It is then a short drive along a narrow rural lane.

The natural cove of the beach at Yellowcraig is an attractive and pristine area backed by dunes, woodland and grassland. It is located a short distance west of North Berwick and is easily reached from Edinburgh by car in under an hour. The beauty of the beach is

further enhanced by the views of the tiny island of Fidra (the inspiration for Robert Louis Stevenson's *Treasure Island*) and its lighthouse, which was erected in 1885.

From the car park, the beach is a short walk through the trees and across the dunes. There is a separate path for dog walkers, and a nature trail runs up the east side of the shore. Large grassy areas with picnic tables provide room to relax.

The ruins of 13th-century Dirleton Castle – with its drawbridge, chapel and pit prison – lie about a mile from Yellowcraig.

Gullane Bents

Take the A1 east from Edinburgh and join the A198 coastal road. Gullane Bents is signposted from the village of Gullane.

Superb views of the Firth of Forth aren't the only aspect Gullane Bents has to offer – an arc of soft golden sand in a beautiful rural setting add to its splendour. *Bent* is an old word for heath or moorland, hence the stark contrast between coast and countryside you'll find here.

This is both a good family attraction and a top bathing spot, making it one of the most popular beaches in the east of Scotland. The shore here is very well managed, with designated walkways to the beach and signposted wheelchair-access

routes across the sand dunes. You'll find picnic tables at the end of the Marine Terrace promenade, and for those who've not brought lunch, the village of Gullane provides a range of eateries.

Twenty miles from Gullane is Scotland's capital, Edinburgh, home each August to the Edinburgh International Festival.

Burntisland

Burntisland is well signposted from the A921, which runs along the coast. The beach and parking are signposted from the centre of Burntisland.

The royal burgh of Burntisland lies on the south coast of Fife, just across the river from Edinburgh. It is located between the Forth Road Bridge and Kirkcaldy, with views across the Firth of Forth, and has long been a popular family seaside resort with the residents

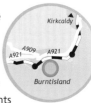

of Fife and the Lothians.

Backed by a promenade, the sandy beach boasts clean bathing water that regularly attract swimmers and paddlers in the summer months. However, this is all a far cry from just a decade ago when Burntisland was one of many Scottish beaches branded a 'national scandal' for its dirty coastal conditions. Today, it is one of the cleanest beaches in Scotland.

Serious ramblers can stretch their legs along the Fife Coastal Path – a real walk on the wild side. This

With this great reputation you might expect the beach to get overcrowded, but the resort is sufficiently large to offer a wealth of entertainment without ever getting too boisterous – even during the summer fairground season. At this time of year the top attractions include the seaside park, bouncy castles, crazy golf and the swimming pool at the Beacon leisure centre, which offers water slides and a wave machine. For the adults, jet-skiing and sailing are available off the coast. Additional facilities include picnic tables, plenty of parking spaces, public toilets and first-aid and lifeguard points.

If you're after a really peaceful setting, nearby Aberdour beach sits in a delightful location and guarantees you a serene spot.

beautiful route runs for over 80 miles from North Queensferry in the south to Newport-on-Tay in the north.

St Andrews, West Sands

St Andrews is well signposted from the west, south and east and is served by the A91, A915 and A917.

On arriving at West Sands beach in St Andrews there is a sign that reads, 'Welcome to West Sands. You are now at one of the busiest beaches in Scotland'. The sign serves two purposes: it praises this stretch of wonderful Fife coastline while at the same time warning you that you'd better be prepared to share towel space. West Sands is the best beach in St Andrews. Clean and well maintained, it offers two miles of wide sandy beach with views of the town and the world-famous golf course. It is also backed by sand dunes bound by marram and lyme grass, which are home to a wide range of wildlife. When it isn't crammed, West Sands is perfect for kids to play beach games on. And it's safe; the beach shelves gently to the water, which is clean and safe for bathers. This is also a great venue for the active – joggers, kite surfers, windsurfers – everyone's invited!

West Sands is famous for appearing in the opening sequence of *Chariots of Fire* as the British Olympic

Beyond the dunes are toilet facilities, a large car park, picnic area and Castles snack bar, which sells hot and cold food as well as ice cream – everything you need to ensure your day at the beach runs smoothly. St Andrews' town centre also has a wide range of shops, bars, restaurants and accommodation.

If you feel like exploring, then East Sands beach, adjacent to the harbour, and Kingsbarns beach, a short distance from St Andrews in a southerly direction along the coast road, are both popular alternatives to West Sands.

St Andrews is home to Scotland's oldest university, but is perhaps better known as being the home of golf. The links course is over 600 years old and there are records of Archbishop John Hamilton confirming the right of local residents to play golf in the 1550s. The Old Course is in fact a public course and, in theory, anybody is eligible to play a round here. However, you may find booking a tee-off time is as difficult as hitting a hole in one.

team train on it. Made in 1981, the film won four Oscars. Sadly, the movie mistakenly credits the scene to Broadstairs in Kent.

Aberdeen

Aberdeen is accessible from the A90 to the north and south and the A93 from the west. The beach is easily reached from the city centre.

Nestling on the coast at the confluence of the rivers Dee and Don, the 'Granite City' is renowned for its ties with the oil industry. However, this lively place also boasts a wonderful and expansive sandy beach that stretches for two miles just north of the city.

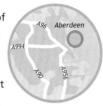

The beach is popular with locals and surfers, who seem to relish braving the cold water, and volunteer lifeguards are on duty during summer. Fishing is also popular here, although it's best to avoid the busy harbour area. Behind the promenade are several nightclubs and a cinema complex, and Aberdeen beach is also home to Scotland's largest permanent funfair.

Nearby Crathes Castle boasts some of Scotland's most spectacular gardens among its gargoyles and battlements.

Redpoint

From Gairloch take the A832 south then turn right onto the B8056 following
signs to Red Point.

Redpoint is a beautiful, remote and pristine
beach located in the Highlands of northwest
Scotland. The nearest settlement of any size
is Gairloch, approximately 10 miles to the
north. From the car park, the beach is reached
along a sheep-nibbled track which leads to the
dunes bordering the shore. The beach is a pristine expanse of
sand, slightly reddish in colour and framed at either end by
rocks – the perfect place to perch with a picnic and marvel at
the bravery of someone taking a dip in the chilly sea.

You may find it difficult to tear yourself away from the
magnificent views of the Cuillin Hills on the Isle of Skye and
the beautiful sunsets. Dogs are allowed on the beach
throughout the year and there is an enticing coastal walk that
starts close by. Due to the remote location, don't forget to
take your own food and drink.

Stop off at the hamlet of Badachro on your departure from
the beach – it offers the first pub of the homeward journey.

Sanna Bay

Follow the B8007 west. Sanna Bay is signposted from Kilchoan on the southern side of the Ardnamurchan Peninsula along mainly unclassified roads.

Without doubt one of Britain's most secluded beaches, Sanna Bay is definitely worth the journey. To illustrate its remoteness, consider this: Ardnamurchan Point, the most westerly point of the British mainland, lies further west than even Land's End in Cornwall. The nearest shop is around six miles away so be sure to take everything you need to keep you occupied and contented! The Ardnamurchan peninsula is very sparsely populated, but animal and plant life thrive in its isolated and unpolluted conditions.

The beach consists of an arc of soft, pristine white sand, which is as likely to be dotted with the footprints of local wildlife as it is with human tracks. You'll find that the shore here is divided

Ardnamurchan is as pure and pristine a place as you'll find in Britain. Ideal for rambling, from the lighthouse you may see

in places by dark rocky outcrops that offer a good selection of rock pools to trawl through for mini marine discoveries.

Behind Sanna Bay is a large area of dunes and grass – home to grazing sheep and numerous bird species. Care should be taken not to deviate from the paths when crossing the dunes, as this is an environmentally sensitive area that is easily damaged.

The nearest major settlement is Fort William, which is a journey by road of around 60 miles – an unforgettable drive through ancient oak forests and meadows of wild flowers. However, Sanna Bay is actually easier to access not by car but by boat – from Tobermory on the Isle of Mull. A short ferry ride takes you to Kilchoan on the peninsula from where it is a drive of around 20 minutes up to Sanna Bay.

whales, basking sharks and dolphins, while red deer, curlew and snipe inhabit the heather moorlands and birch woods.

Calgary Bay

From the ferry terminal at Craignure take the A849 and turn left after Salen onto the single-track road to Dervaig. Join the B8073 and continue west to Calgary Bay.

Calgary Bay is a beautiful rural beach on the Isle of Mull, Scotland's third largest island. It is considered by many to be one of the finest beaches in the country. Part of the attraction is its isolated location – right on the island's west coast – combined with the surrounding dramatic, rugged scenery.

From the bay's two small car parks it is a short walk to the beach, where soft, silvery white sand is dotted with shells and occasional patches of rocks. Bathing is considered safe as the

bay is relatively sheltered and the beach shelves very gently into the sea, which is beautifully clear. The shore is backed by dunes and fertile grasslands that support a

A trip to the island wouldn't be complete without visiting the Mull Theatre in Dervaig. In a small converted barn seating just

wide variety of plants and wildlife. This environmentally sensitive area is at the mercy of heavy Atlantic storms, grazing sheep, and people enjoying the beach, so please take care when spending the day here. For walkers, the path through the beech trees of Calgary Wood steers you past a restored millpond, a derelict sawmill and some interesting sculptures.

Tobermory is the island's capital and is a 20-minute drive from the beach along the narrow, winding roads of the B8073. Be aware that this is tantamount to a road roller coaster, with its twisting turns and crazy contours. However, numerous shops and restaurants along Tobermory's attractive natural harbour mean it's a good place to eat or stock up on supplies before heading for a day at the beach – worth remembering if you decide to drive all the way up the coast road from Craignure.

you and the 42 others in the audience, a professional theatre group presents a new programme each season.

Index

Page numbers are shown in **bold**.